#GOOD FOR NOTHING NALAYAK

hilarious short stories for the Indian soul

A Mistake
by
Shiva Shankar Iyer

First published in 2018
by Becomeshakespeare.com
Wordit Content Design & Editing Services Pvt Ltd
Unit - 26, Building A-1, Nr Wadala RTO, Wadala (East),
Mumbai 400037, India
T:+91 8080226699

This book has been funded by WORDIT ART FUND
WORDIT ART FUND helps deserving
Authors publish their work
To apply for funding, please visit us at
becomeshakespeare.com

Copyright © 2018 by Shiva Shankar Iyer
All rights reserved. Any unauthorized reprint or use of this material is prohibited. No part of this book may be reproduced or transmitted in any form or by any means, electronic or mechanical, including photocopying, recording, or by any information storage and retrieval system without express written permission from the author/publisher. Please do not participate in or encourage piracy of copyrighted materials in violation of the author's rights. Purchase only authorized editions.

©
ISBN : 978-93-87649-21-7

Disclaimer:
This is a work of fiction. Names, characters, business, place, event and incidents are either the product of the author's imagination or used in a fictitious manner. Any resemblance to actual person, living or dead or actual event is purely coincidental.

DEDICATION

mother, Lakshmi Shankar Iyer
father, Shankar Iyer
brother, Hari Shankar Iyer
Friends.
Teachers.
Critics who couldn't take a joke.

ACKNOWLEDGEMENTS

"This is SHIT," said my friend, after reading one of my stories.

"Why bro?" I asked teary eyed.

"Try Chetan Bhagat. He can be your inspiration."

Thank You Sir, for your delightful words.

First off, a big hug and thank you to everyone who has ever criticised my work. I believe the growth of an author is in the brickbats, not in the accolades.

My Alma Mater: The Brigade School and Kumarans, in the Silicon City of India. The dream of becoming an author nurtured from here. Thank you to all my teachers, who have taught me more about life than academics.

A shout out to my school and college friends, who have continuously encouraged my writing skills through Facebook likes and shares. Special thanks to Alip, Niranjan and Arvind for being extremely judgemental of my work; Sahana and Kedar for the critical feedback; and Sailesh Shahri for the free rides on his Honda Activa.

Arnav, Ashish, Shashank, Ragul, Rajeev, Sushi: you guys made school worthwhile.

The blind reviews given by my family and friends.

A lot of people have been part of this amazing journey – I may have not mentioned their names here. Sorry guys. Nevertheless, you know who you are. Thank You.

My parents, Shankar and Lakshmi; and brother Hari for their unflinching support in reviewing, editing and the in-your-face comments for the book. I have enjoyed the 'tea- biscuit-argument' sessions in the evenings immensely.

The WordIT team, for giving me an amazing opportunity to present my thoughts to the world.

The Almighty.

Last, and obviously not the least: Microsoft Word. I would personally love to thank Bill Gates, so I will be sending my work as an e-book to him.

He can read it on his iPad.

ABOUT THE AUTHOR

Shiva Shankar Iyer is currently pursuing his second year of Engineering from The National Institute of Engineering, Mysuru (Mysore) in Karnataka. His work has been published twice in Young World - the supplement for youngsters from The Hindu, a leading daily. He has been dabbling in writing since the past 5 years.

In addition to writing humour based content, his work has been published on technical topics such as Digilocker and Self Driving Cars.

He has sailed through 12th standard with decent marks to keep pestering relatives at bay. Apart from writing, Shiva has won medals at National Level Abacus Competitions and is an avid fan of debating and public speaking.

CONTENTS

Part 1: *School's Out!*

1.	9 to 10	1
2.	The Facebook Funda	3
3.	No IIT, No Wife	6
4.	Parent Teacher Meetings	9
5.	Just Chilling	12
6.	Counselling: A Beginner's Guide	14
7.	Turning 18	17
8.	The Khadoos Indian Parent	19

Part 2: *College Life & etc.*

1.	Hostel Life – Part 1: The Beginning	23
2.	Hostel Life – Part 2: Exams	25
3.	ID Card	41
4.	The Dilemma with buying Fruits and Vegetables	43

5.	Finding a Girlfriend	47
6.	Pickup Lines	49
7.	Complimenting a Girl	52
8.	Mass Bunk: The Power of an Idea	58

Part 3: Kabhi Logic, Kabhi Hum

1.	Chaos in the Kitchen	65
2.	To Jog *or* Not to Jog?	68
3.	*Bas Karo* Traffic!	72
4.	Google Maps, Where are You?	75
5.	The Love for Food *or* Love and Food?	80
6.	What's your Name again?	83
7.	Bro, where's the Treat?	85
8.	Economics: A Dummies Guide	87
9.	Management Lessons from Wife	89
10.	North Indians Vs South Indians	90
11.	Maid in India	93
12.	Keep the Change: The One Rupee Revolution	97
13.	Writing to the Devil	104
14.	Raksha Bandhan	112

Part 4: Travel Diaries

1.	Buttering the Dosa : A trip to North Karnataka	115
2.	Call of the Cholas : The Tanjavur Diaries	118
3.	Call of the Halwa : The Tirunelveli Diaries Part 1	129
4.	The Hunger Games: The Tirunelveli Diaires Part 2	134

PART 1

SCHOOL'S OUT!

Chapter 1

9 TO 10

The crowd cheers as fireworks adorn the sky with its exuberant colours. I run across the field, screaming out of joy. Never had I felt this good before. My dream of captaining the Indian team to victory and lifting the Cricket World Cup trophy had finally been fulfilled…

Or so I thought.

Suddenly, amidst all these celebrations, I heard a ring which sounded like the infamous bell in our school. Time froze. I was jerked out of my bed by such a strong force that I couldn't even think of having an extra minute of sleep, and that force was none other than my father. I complained that I was tired from my celebrations last night. My father gave me a stern look, signifying that I better get ready for school or else… well, you know the implications.

Personally, I think that my family has our very own version of the Olympic field at home. I dodge my brother, making a fiery 100m dash towards the main door, my father jumping at the rustling of the morning newspaper, while my mother stood in the kitchen, relaying messages across all the rooms. In all this confusion, my head started to swim.

Subtle.

"Have I done my homework?" "Have I irritated my brother?" "Have I forgotten what I remembered and remembered what I had forgotten?" Such thoughts cloud my mind while I wait at the bus stop. I smile in satisfaction as I tick each item off my checklist. A beautiful start to a perfect day.

After a brief hour of sleep in the bus, I wake up to find myself in class, left at the mercy of algebra and atoms.

The eagerly awaited short break arrives. We eat, we chat and we laugh. The next part of the day rushes past like a blizzard, and I find myself at home, either completing my homework or playing football in the grounds. Arriving home, the whole house becomes a complete "study centre". I oblige the couch and sit in front of the television from 9 to 10 pm after which exhaustion takes over.

This, ladies and gentlemen, is one day in my life.

Chapter 2

THE FACEBOOK FUNDA

I had finally joined Facebook in my 10th standard, much to the relief of my friends, who had termed me as "better late than never". I was excited at the prospect of catching up with old friends, retaining present ones and making fresh acquaintances.

But after a few days............well, see for yourself.

When I finished the usual registrations and clicked "Log in", I felt a certain thrill run through me. At last, I wouldn't be the black sheep in the pack. At last, I would be the first person to know when everyone was going for a cricket match. At last, I would know when we had a Math exam instead of Social Studies. It's really the small things here and there that count the most.

Logging in for the first time is like sending an open signal to every single person online. The moment I logged in, 10 friend requests popped up on my wall. I accepted them gracefully, and moved on to look at the different features of Facebook. Thus, the entire day was spent in accepting requests, replying to "Welcome to FB!!!!!!!!" messages and looking at friend's pictures in various poses.

A great man once said:

"A person's Facebook wall is like a public urinal. Everyone comes here, posts whatever they want and moves on."

I couldn't agree more.

Even more, people kept updating their statuses on every other thing on the planet. "It's raining!" – 10 likes. "Heavy rains!" – 22 likes. "It's finally raining! – 30 likes. Even the Meteorological Department checks Facebook for the weather forecast.

But yes, Facebook does have its own set of merits. It allows us to connect with family members or friends abroad easily and even allows us to participate in various competitions hosted by companies, as every start-up has now moved towards Facebook in order to garner support for their product and create a fan following online.

As I browsed through the news feed, I remembered an interesting conversation pertaining to Facebook. Excerpts:

Note: Names changed for fear of prosecution.

"Hey Divya! Did you come online yesterday?"
"Nah. Too busy studying."

"Hmmmm............ok. When you go online today, go to my page and like the photo which I had posted yesterday. I'm wearing a red shirt, so also comment on how good I look in that shirt."

I instinctively looked away as I had a hard time suppressing my laughter. Both the girls looked at me at once. I managed to keep a straight face and said –"Jolly good weather, eh?" in *pakka* British style.

"*Teri tho*......," said one of the girls.

The entire text cannot be reproduced here due to non-approval from the Censor Board.

I didn't know Hindi at that time, so I kept smiling.

As I was about to log out, I noticed the chat notification. It had a speech bubble with a "1". I clicked on it and behold –I started chatting with my friend for about an hour or so until I decided that the *rajma* (red kidney beans) in the kitchen was more enticing than prolonging a boring conversation. I logged out (finally) and marched into the kitchen.

Facebook was great for a day.....................
But going online everyday?
No thanks.

Chapter 3

NO IIT, NO WIFE

Every single self respecting 11th and 12th grade Science student would have gone through this phase. The phase which has defined the future of millions of students in the Indian subcontinent.

The IIT Phase.

In India, whenever relatives come home, after all the initial greetings and when your jaw starts hurting from smiling:

"*Ya ya*, everyone's fine. So Shiva, which class are you in now?" Latha Aunty asked.

"Aunty I just finished 10th. My board exams got over a week ago." I grinned.

Latha Aunty frowned.

"Oh. So what are you doing in your holidays?"

I started talking like a tape recorder."Swimming, cricket, eating, sleeping, movies, going to……."

Aunty put up her hand. I shut up immediately.

She turned to my mother.

"Lakshmi, what's this? Shouldn't he be in IIT coaching? You should enroll him tomorrow itself. Swimming *gimming* is all okay, but he should start studying now. What say?"

See, I was pretty clear that I wanted to get into the country's best for Engineering. I also knew that getting into IIT was a great idea, because of the opportunities and the people that one gets exposed to.

But during the 10th holidays? This was too much.

The very next day, my parents and I set off to my senior's place to get "IIT material". She had just finished her 12th in the Science group, but was keen on getting an Economics degree. She had put out a mail saying that her books were available for sale.

So we landed up at her house.

When people say:

"I have many cars," - it obviously means that they have about two or three.

Or when people say: "I ate 10 laddoos, they were THAT big," (exaggerated hand gesture), you can tell that they had about 4 or 5.

But when my senior had said that she had a FEW books up for grabs, doesn't mean she can put her entire bookshelf for sale.

"So these are my reference books, my IIT coaching books, my question paper books, answer book for question paper book, formula book……." she rambled on.

I ran away from that place.

A week later, another relative visited our house. This time it was my father's friend who had come home. He had studied with my father in Kota, Rajasthan. Once he had downed six *jalebis* (an Indian sweet) and three cups of tea:

He took me aside and told:

"IIT *karo beta*, otherwise no IIT, no wife."

How far this is true, I don't know.

Chapter 4

PARENT TEACHER MEETINGS

Everyone hates Parent Teacher Meetings.

By everyone, I mean the teachers, parents and especially the students.

That one day, when we are forced to wear our school uniforms and put on a grin as we walk with our parents to the meeting room.

"It's going to be a terrible day," I tell myself.

It's always awkward when you see your friends with their parents. When I meet them during school hours, I'd say:

"Eh Karthik, where you died for so many days?"

But now:

"Oh hi aunty, how are you? Yes, I'm fine, thank you. Oh this is Karthik? Ha ha ha that's very nice. We hardly get to talk in school, you know."

LOL.

Anyway,

I wait for my name to be called. I hadn't done a great job with my marks in the terminal exams, so I was bound to face the music.

"Shiva," the teacher called out.

I reluctantly sat in the chair opposite the teacher as my father took the remaining chair next to mine. I was in direct line of the firing squad.

Sunita Ma'am gave me a plastic smile. I swear I had seen that smile somewhere in a horror movie.

"So Shiva, not doing well nowadays hmmm?"

As if she didn't know.

"Heh heh yes ma'am......"

My father jumped in: "Ma'am, what is the problem? Why is he not scoring any marks? I see him studying everyday, but there are no results to show it!"

Sunita Ma'am calmly said:

"He has to put in more effort. Hardwork is required."

But my father wasn't convinced.

"No but where EXACTLY should he put in the hardwork??"

"You have to give more time to studies." she repeated.

"Ma'am please tell him where to improve!"

"Study for more hours, see what happens."

What do you mean 'see what happens'? I have some very good advice I would love to give Sunita Ma'am.

Stand in front of a speeding car, see what happens. If you can fly it's ok.

My father was clearly frustrated now. He said in a very civilised way - "Thank you very much Ma'am, for your time."

I waved to my friend at the nearby table. By the look on his face, he too was facing a lot of music.

As I heaved a sigh of relief, sensing the end of the meeting, Sunita Ma'am responded to a phone call asking her to attend *her* daughter's Parent Teacher's meeting tomorrow.

Something about low marks and more hardwork required.

Life is a beautiful cycle.

Chapter 5

JUST CHILLING

There's a huge divide between the previous generations and the present one. This story will address these issues.

One fine day some elderly relatives had come home.

If American relatives came home:

"Oh yeah yeah, so what's Bill Gates up to?" They'd ask me.

If Indian relatives came home:

"Beta IIT *karo*."

Anyway,

"So beta, how were your exams?" they asked me.

"Cool," I replied.

"Cool means....?" they asked me suspiciously.

"Ummm....cool means? Cool means...they went well," I stammered.

"Ok ok. So what are you doing in your holidays?"

"Chilling," I said.

"Now what is this CHILLING? Where are you chilling, in the fridge?" he almost shouted.

"No no no, it means that I'm relaxing, playing cricket, seeing movies etc etc."

"You kids nowadays.......so what do you do most of the time?"

"I'm on FB."

Whatever happened next, use your imagination.

Chapter 6

COUNSELLING: A BEGINNER'S GUIDE

What exactly is Counselling?

The first thing that comes to my mind is a person sitting with you, coaxing you to open up and trying to solve your life's problem.

But in my 12th standard, I came across a different type of Counselling - Seat Counselling.

It's very simple. Basically you choose your Engineering seat based on the rank that you have secured in that particular exam.

In simple terms:

Let's say you are at a restaurant. You walk in and take your seat.

You call the waiter and ask:

"Sir, what's on the menu?"

"*Idly, vada, kara bath, masala dosa, plain dosa, butter masala, poori, chole batura.....*" he drones on.

Now, if you get a good rank in your exam:

"Okay okay stop. Gimme a masala dosa and a poori."

"Okay Sir!" the waiter takes your order.

But if you get a bad rank in your exam:

"Sir, what's on the menu?"

" Plain dosa, tea, coffee." he says.

"What?! No masala dosa, poori....????"

The waiter gives you a sheepish smile.

"Sorry sir, there's no masala, because the person who came before you had the last helping."

"Hmm...what about the poori?" you ask.

Waiter again gives a sheepish smile.

"Heh heh, sorry sir, there is no oil left for the pooris. If you want we can fry it in water sir," he replies.

Your anger meter is nearing red at the waiter's cheekiness.

"We have coffee and tea. Which one would you like to have? Sir please tell fast, there are 10 other people asking for tea."

"Give me bloody tea."

"Right sir!" the waiter rushes to the kitchen

After you're done with your tea, the waiter starts walking towards you in a suspicious way.

He bends down towards you and whispers:

"Sir, you asked for poori right? I can get it for you easily. But...." his sentence hangs in the air.

"But what?" you ask.

"But...it'll cost you slightly extra. 50 rupees more sir."

So what does this imply?

If you have a good rank, you choose the item.

If you don't, let the item choose you.

Bhaihyon, behno: this is Counselling :)

Chapter 7

TURNING 18

Turning 18 is one of the most awaited moments in a teen's life.

We officially become adults! We're no longer "that little kid playing on the slide."

When I was about 15, my older cousins used to take me around in their motorbikes. I asked them whether I could ride too.

They laughed and said - "Wait till you turn 18."

It was election time. I was walking on the road when I saw the local politician campaigning in my colony.

I ran up to him and asked - "When can I threaten you with my vote?"

He laughed and said - "Wait till you turn 18."

Some relatives had come home.

"Awwww...he's such a small boy! Just look at his face. Sooo innocent."

"Aunty I'm 17. Tomorrow's my birthday. I'm not a small child anymore."

She laughed and said - "Wait till you turn 18."

About time.

We can finally roam the streets as an adult, take our own decisions and make our own choices. Technically we should be out of the house, but let's not bring that up.

All this while, our parents have told us about the big, bad world that's waiting to grab us in its clutches. But now, we're officially IN the big bad world.

Not to worry. Eighteen's a beautiful age. New beginnings, new opportunities await.

But you know the worst part about turning 18?

"Uncle, uncle - how to go to Jayanagar? My mummy's waiting there," a little girl asked me.

Chapter 8

THE KHADOOS INDIAN PARENT

Indian parents mean well................generally speaking.

They want only the best for their children, and nothing less than the best will do.

"Which is why I've decided that my son is going to join an engineering college," Sharma uncle said proudly.

"But uncle.....Akshay wanted to pursue a course in Music right? He was bent upon joining a music academy, even the scholarship letter had arrived......" I said timidly.

"Are you his father? Or am I?" Sharma uncle glared at me.

"Shall we do a paternity test?" I thought to myself.

"Anyway, this '3 Idiots' movie is spoiling the entire youth of this country. 'Follow your Passion',

'Do what you love'.................all nonsense. If Akshay does not do Engineering, how will he get married?"

Girls married only engineers? I did not know that.

"By 25 he should get married, by 27 he should have his first kid, and by 29 - the second kid should be on its way," he said teary eyed.

"Uncle, this is not *Dhoom* Series, 2 movies in 2 years," I murmured to myself.

"How I wish to become a grandfather....."

"Uncle, how is Akshay's music album going? I heard it's going to become a hit!"

".......And by 30, invest in some shares, mutual funds, and earn some extra income through fixed deposits. Life is set," Sharma uncle continued, completely ignoring my previous statement.

"How boring," my eyes started to close.

"But more importantly.........WAKE UP!" he shouted suddenly.

"Huh?! Sorry I am all ears – Please continue."

"More importantly, I want my children to continue my legacy." he said emotionally.

Who did he think he was? King Ashoka?

Later in the day, I happened to run across Akshay in the local grocery store.

"Hi Akshay! Long time!" I said cheerfully.

"I know! How are you?"

"I'm fine. I met your father today."

His expression suddenly became sombre.

"So, *Dhoom 1* and its sequel are on the way, eh?" I joked.

"Bro, I've decided to invest in mutual funds."

"What?!" I said, my mouth open in utter shock.

"What about music? What about the World Tour? What about the screaming fans? This was your dream!" I continued.

Akshay took out a piece of paper from his pocket. It had a few lines written on it, with his father's sign below. I snatched it from him, and read it out loud –

"Music is subject to market risks. Please donate your guitar and your soul carefully before investing."

PART 2

COLLEGE LIFE AND ETC.

Chapter 1

HOSTEL LIFE – PART 1: THE BEGINNING

When I was in my 12th standard, I used to imagine how it would be going to college. Chilling out, having fun, last minute studying, bunking classes and so on.

My seniors used to talk about life in a hostel. It seemed very exciting. Think about it - nobody to tell you to iron your uniform, or eat on time or study when exams are near. You have a certain independence to yourself.

But jokes apart, I did not expect hostel life to be like this.

On the first day, when I got up from my bed, I found my bucket missing and my balcony door open. I had class at 7:30 am and I had got up at 7:15 am.

Shakespeare had once written - "To be or not to be."

Right now I had to decide - "To bathe or not to bathe."

I figured that my hostel mates next door would have taken it. Our rooms are interconnected by a balcony, and the partition between the rooms is almost a metre and a half high. I pieced together that someone in the next room was possessed by Spider Man and had jumped over and taken my bucket.

Thank God deodorants were invented. (Don't tell my parents)

It's my first week right? New college, new people, new FOOD. And new is not necessarily good. When I first went to the college mess in the afternoon, I said:

"*Bhaiya* one meals."

He stared at me for a minute, eyes unwavering. I was getting nervous, so I started to count the number of chapatis in the room for no reason. Finally, he placed 3 cups in front of me.

Cup Number 1: Vegetable curry.

Correction: Cannot Say.

Cup Number 2: Sambar

Correction: Some orange thing which looked like it had done some sin in its past life and landed here.

Cup Number 3: Curd

Correction: Take thick curd, dilute it up to 10 times by adding tap water and serve cold. Add salt if available.

I miss home food:(

Chapter 2

HOSTEL LIFE - PART 2: EXAMS

Look back at your life. Introspect deeply.

Look back 20 years, 30 years or even 5 days ago.

What is the toughest thing you have ever done?

Have you climbed Mount Everest?

Piece of cake. Vanilla cake.

Have you dived with Sharks?

Easy.

Have you survived a hostel's mess food?

Been there, done that.

But, have you ever studied in a hostel room during your final exams?

It is the toughest thing to do in the world.

I am in a three sharing room. A three sharing room mean 3 times the madness during exam time.

"*Macha*, Maths exam is in 3 days. Pass your notes da, I need to study," said Pratik, my roommate number one.

We had our first exam coming up: Mathematics.

"No chance. I have to revise the trigonometry formulae. Why don't you ask Rajath?"

Rajath was one of the toppers of our hostel. By topper I mean, he was a 9 CGPA out of 10 guy, which was not an easy feat to achieve in our college.

"Bro, Rajath has been absconding for a week now. Legend has it that he comes out exactly at 12 pm midnight to have his dinner. He has locked himself up in the college campus to study, I don't know where though," Pratik said thoughtfully.

"Even ghosts have punctuality that these mess fellows don't have," I murmured to myself.

"What?"

"Nothing bro, Just revising the formulae again," I smiled sheepishly.

"Bro, atleast tell me the portions for the test," Pratik pleaded.

"Sure that I can tell,"

I rattled off like a parrot.

"Integration, Differentiation, Matrices....."

"Mattresses?"

"Matrices."

"Bro my mattress is fine. I have to change it anyway. Too many bed bugs," Pratik said.

"Bed bugs???" I exclaimed, startled.

There was a moment of silence.

"How the hell is this guy going to become an engineer, he doesn't even know what Matrices is," I thought to myself.

"How the hell is this going to become an engineer, he doesn't even know what Bed Bugs are," Pratik thought to himself.

"Anyway – there's Matrices, Conic Sections and Tracing of Curves."

"That's it?"

"Are you mad? Conic Sections take one day to finish, tracing of curves about half a day, and don't even get me started on integration and differentiation. You're in a big mess, my friend." I counselled Pratik.

"Bro, try to enjoy life. You live only once. You want some Parle-G biscuits?" Pratik said.

This is the situation of future engineers in our country.

***

In a hostel, or anywhere for that matter, during exam time, there are 3 kinds of people you will come across:

TYPE 1:

People who have finished all the portions, and are thorough with each and every chapter, but act as though they are looking at the chapter for the first time.

Please Note: Names have been changed to maintain professional integrity.

Me : "Raju, I have a doubt in this problem. Can you solve it for me?"

Raju : (looking at the problem intently for a few seconds) "Bro, what chapter is this?"

Me : (perplexed) Matrices.

If Rajath was a 9 CGPA guy, Raju was a 9.5 CGPA holder. I was shocked he didn't know about Matrices 3 days before the final exams.

Raju : "What?"

Me : "Matrices," I repeated.

Raju : "Mattresses? Do you want one?"

Me : "No dude, its MATRICES! You put numbers inside brackets……"

Raju : "Is it? My God, I haven't even touched that chapter yet. Give me 3 days time- I will explain it to you."

Me : "3 DAYS? The exam is in 3 days!"

Raju : (shrugging his shoulders) "That's the best I can do."

I walked away from his room with a swollen face.

"You think I don't know what Matrices is? I've done a PhD on that subject. Just as there can be only one King in the Jungle, there can be only one Maths

Topper in this hostel!" Raju thought triumphantly to himself.

TYPE 2:

People who have just started studying, and will not be disturbed at any cost.

"Bro, I have a doubt." I said.

"Go away, I'm studying," Kiran responded, without looking up from his Maths textbook.

"Bro, please," I pleaded.

"Don't disturb, I'm studying," Kiran said.

"Bro you'll fail this time also, it's ok - stop studying."

"Get lost."

"Bro come for lunch."

"Bro I'm busy here!"

"Bro I'm going to Mars."

"Go and come fast, get some coriander and green tea."

"Bro I'm setting your room on fire."

"Sure, it was cold here anyway."

"Bro here are the spoilers of Game Of Thrones next episode."

"Ok what doubt you have?" Kiran relented.

You should know everyone's weakness during exams. For example, Raju cannot resist Pani Puri, and Rajath cannot resist buttering.

"So Rajath, I heard you're studying hard for the exams." I said.

"No bro, nothing like that, I haven't even started," Rajath grins.

I shot an arrow from my armoury.

"Come on *yaar*, we all know that you're going to top the college this time too! I mean, there's no one else better than you when it comes to academics!"

"*Arre* nothing like that….."

The above sentence translated to: "Tell me more."

"Teachers come to you for doubts! What would they be without you," I massaged his ego.

"Heh heh, you are too kind," Rajath started to blush.

There is always a one second window in which you have to pounce on the opportunity at hand.

"So……Rajath…I had this doubt in Maths. You know, in Matrices?"

By this time, the barricade had fallen.

"Matrices? *Arre voh toh easy hai!* (That is very easy!) Tell me, what is your doubt?"

Me -1, Rajath -0.

TYPE 3:

People who will not study at all, and will not let you study.

"Bro, let's go for a movie," my second roommate, Nitin said.

"Dude, we have a Math exam in 3 days. Better buck up and start studying," I retorted.

"Dude, C'mon man……..it's a Spiderman movie," Nitin tried to put his point across.

"Spiderman, Batman, any man, I cannot and will not go for the movie. Please let me study in peace."

"You come for the movie NOW, or else……" his voice lingered on menacingly.

"Or WHAT?" my eyes pierced into his soul.

"Watch out!" he screamed.

Like the genius I am, I covered my head. As I covered my head, I could not see my Maths textbook being snatched away by Nitin.

"Yaaaassss!!!!" he shouted triumphantly, and ran outside the room.

I chased him, but the Fried Rice and Chocolate ice-cream from last night weighed me down.

I went to the room adjacent to mine.

"Avi, I need your Math textbook."

"No dude, I need to study!" Avi exclaimed.

"I'll Xerox it and give it back."

"Xerox will easily take an hour. I can't take that risk." Avi said.

"Look there!" I pointed my finger in the upward direction.

"Where?? What happened?"

By the time Avi figured out what was going on, I had taken his math textbook and hid in another friend's room.

"*Yaar* Sonu, I have Avi's textbook. Tell him you never saw me." I gave my instructions.

"Ok, no issues." Sonu assured me.

I could trust Sonu. He was the only person living in a three sharing room, and people hardly came over here, because Sonu had made it very clear that he valued his privacy more than anything else.

I valued my sanity more than anything else.

I studied in peace for the next 5 hours. I had completed 3 chapters in that time duration, and was extremely happy with my progress. I was planning to revise the last 2 chapters at night, and then practice some question papers the next day.

Until this happened.

"Bro, Sonu, let's go to the bakery for some tea." I said.

"Hmm… coming." Sonu was occupied in an Integration sum.

"Dude, let's go. I'm hungry." I begged.

"Half an hour," Sonu murmured.

"Look there!" I screamed at the top of my voice.

"Shivaaaa!!!! Is that youuuu???"

Shit.

Avi had discovered my hideout.

"*Haan*, Shiva is here only! Come and get him!" Sonu smiled at me in evil glee as he opened the door of his room.

"*Et tu* Sonu?" I thought to myself.

So my current situation was, I had no math textbook, I had 2 chapters to revise, and I had been backstabbed by my good(now bad) friend.

I whipped out my phone and called my roommate.

"Hello Nitin? You went for the movie?"

"Oh still haven't gone? Great! Book one ticket for me also."

***

It was the last day before the Maths Exam. Everyone had spent two out of three days wasting their time on their respective phones watching the India Vs Pakistan cricket match, Big Boss and Balika Vadhu.

But there was only one day left. Everyone was frantically trying to cover up the portions for the test.

The smart guys were going through last year's question papers, studying the important questions and well, praying to God.

"God, if I pass this test, I will break 108 coconuts daily."

"God, if I pass this test, I will do exercise daily."

"God, I pass this test, I will get not take selfies anymore in the bathroom."

And so on and so forth.

"So, this question can come, and this one is also probable, because they've asked this question in the 2014, 2015 and 2016 paper." I noted.

"This is a ten marker question. I can get atleast 5 marks in this one." Rishav murmured.

"Try for ten, this is an easy one."

"Bro, I just want to pass. That's all. I need 40% marks, and then I'm out of the exam hall."

I was shocked, and impressed at his confidence during this time of crisis.

"Hi boys, what are you guys doing? All set?" Rajath walked into my room.

My room door had been open all this while. Rajath usually came into my room to check how much of the portions I had finished.

"Going on, going on. We're solving past years question papers." I replied.

Rajath examined the 2016 question paper for a while.

"Bro, this question is a sure shot one. It is going to come in the exam tomorrow, no doubt," Rajath said.

"Rajath, this sum has never come in any other past paper. What are the chances?" I observed.

"Bro, *chill maar*. Trust me. Sir told us in class."

Rishav and I nodded our heads in agreement, because:

1. Rajath sat in the first bench in class.
2. He noted down everything the teacher uttered.
3. He was the teacher's pet.
4. The milk in the kettle was about to boil, hence I didn't have any time to argue.

***

Time flew with its mighty wings.

Our exam was scheduled at 10 am in the morning. Psychology and common sense dictates that a student must have atleast 8 hours of sleep before an exam.

But we are engineers. Psychology and common sense do not apply to us.

I still had one and half chapters to revise. I would revise it in the morning. I set an alarm for 5 am.

Readers, there is a fundamental thing to understand while reading this story.

If you are at home, and your exam is tomorrow, your parents would probably say:

"It's ok, whatever you have studied – it is more than enough, stop now. Go to sleep, it is already 10pm. Wake up at 6 am and revise all the chapters before going to the exam."

"But Mom, I still have 3 chapters to go!" you would say.

"Marks are only a number, beta. There is more to life than marks or grades. Go to sleep now," she would say in a soothing voice.

But I was in a hostel. The situation would be completely different.

"Dude its only 10 pm – already sleeping?" my friend asked rhetorically as he pulled my blanket.

"QWSDCCZX…….let me be." I said, in my half sleepy state.

"Get up. Teach me Conic sections."

"Get lost."

"You can't sleep now anyway. Look at your room," he said as he pushed me off my bed.

I couldn't open my eyes for about 5 seconds. The tube light's bright light shone directly on my face. There were easily ten people in my room, all chattering and bustling around, trying to compare their class topper's notes and formulae. Someone was teaching a group of five on how to draw a curve.

"So you draw a curve like thiiiiiiiiiiiiiiiis," he stretched the last word like a rubber band, as he sketched out a beautiful curve in his notebook.

"This is a parabola," he continued.

"*Hajmola*?" someone said from the group.

"Parabola, dude – parabola. Haven't you listened in class?"

"We had math class?"

In the middle of all this, I was trying to get some shut-eye. It was like sleeping in a war zone.

A war zone, where you've already lost the war.

Anyway, I had finished teaching my friend Conic Sections.

He yawned lazily.

"Thanks dude, I don't know what I would have done without you," he held my shoulder in gratitude.

"Obviously," I thought to myself.

"Time to sleep," I said.

"Good morning bro," my friend grinned.

"Good morning to you too! What a d….wait. What did you say?"

"I said, good morning." He repeated in an irritated tone.

"What's the time?" I asked, my head spinning.

"The time?" he looked at his watch.

"3:30 am. Or rather, 3:32 am to be precise."

3:30 am? I had kept an alarm for 5 am.

That means I had just one and a half hours of sleep. Which means it was 6 and a half hours of sleep less than what common sense had suggested. But because we are engineers, we can handle 6 hours of sleep. But one and a half hours of sleep were still less than 6 hours of sleep. If I don't get enough sleep, I cannot write the Maths exam with full concentration. I could imagine myself sleeping in the exam, with the question paper as my pillow.

"Let me sleep," I tell the invigilator.

"No, give me your paper," he yanks my answer sheet.

"No no, please don't – I was teaching my friend Conic Sections."

"Bro, don't worry bro, Conic Sections is not there for the test." I heard a voice in the distance.

"Rajath, go way – I want to sleep….no….I have to get up….the math test…"

"Look there!"

"Huh?!"

"Thanks for the paper bro. Now you will definitely fail the test. This time, I will top the Math test. I will reign supreme."

The invigilator had turned into Raju.

"Raju! No please….I will give you Pani Puri…."

I fainted on the spot, my head slamming into the Algebra notes in my room.

***

"Shiva! Wake up! It's 9:00 am! There's only an hour for the exam! How much do you want to sleep?" Nitin shouted in my ear.

"Raju wants Pani Puri, I'm failing my Math test….."

"No silly, the math test is in an hour. Get ready, fast."

I jumped out of my bed, energized. It was only a dream! Thank God, the nightmare was over.

I got dressed, had my breakfast, went through my Cheat Notes of the one and a half chapters I had left, and went to the exam hall, confident as ever.

"Everyone please check your pockets for any chits of paper, phones or any kind of gadget. You will be debarred from writing the exam if you have been found to have any of the items that I have mentioned right now," the invigilator said in a monotonous voice.

I checked my pant pockets. Nothing there.

"Confidence, Shiva – confidence. You got this." I repeated to myself.

The invigilator distributed the question papers, and the moment I laid eyes on the questions, I yelped in delight. "This is going to be one easy test," I thought to myself.

The bell rang, and the exam started.

I started solving the sums at a furious pace. I had not noticed the examination squad walk in.

They started checking everyone's pencil boxes, pouches and calculators for any kind of written material or hints which might help the students cheat in the exam.

The squad reached my desk.

I couldn't care less. I didn't have any chits on me.

"You, stand up," one of the squad members said.

I didn't look up. I assumed he was talking to someone else. I continued to solve my question paper.

"I said, STAND UP!" he pulled me by my shirt and forced me on my feet.

"Sir?! What is going on?" I said, perplexed.

"What is in your shirt pocket?"

"Shirt pocket!? Nothing Sir, you can check...." he slid his fingers into my shirt pocket.

He pulled out a piece of paper.

"Admit One – The Spiderman Movie." It read.

Chapter 3

ID CARD

I was about to stride into my college campus when I was stopped by the security guard.

"Where is your ID Card?" he asked.

"I forgot it at home," I said arrogantly.

He smiled wickedly. "If that's the case, your home is your college today."

Anger erupted inside me. I was already late for class.

I broke into rhyme:
"Its 7:30 in the morning - look at the time,"
"Have some pity, the bell hasn't yet chimed!"
"We students have it tough, only we do know,"
"Wearing an ID card, for all pomp and show!"
"An ID card is important – but I'm late for class,"

"Can we discuss this later, have some *chai* in a glass!"

The security guard retorted:
"Students! Ha!"

"Yours is a carefree generation, I don't deny"
"But with some discipline, one can fly!"
"We're only doing our job, it's our duty to check,"

"Wear an ID Card! It's easier than signing a cheque!"
"We stand in the Sun, come rain or shine,"
"And here you enter! With no sense of time!"
"I will stop you, come what may,"
"Be it now, later: or everyday!"

I humbly salute the security at the entrances of all college campuses.
Thank you for keeping the student community safe.

Chapter 4

THE DILEMMA WITH BUYING FRUITS AND VEGETABLES

Macha, I have a problem.

How on EARTH do you differentiate coriander, *methi* and spinach?

All 3 are green, and all three have........leaves.

One fine day, my mom gave me a list of groceries to buy:

1. Banana
2. Mustard
3. MTR Rava Idly Mix
4. Urad Dal 1/2 kg
5. Towar Dal 1/2 kg
6. Chilli powder 100g
7. Coriander

See, I've noticed one thing. Our generation, be it boys or girls, can talk about Trump, demonetization, India Vs Pakistan Cricket Match and why Marvel is better than DC.

But when it comes to the matters of the kitchen, we have ZERO knowledge.

It's true.

Open your kitchen cupboard, name atleast 5 spices without using Google.

We can eat well, but we can't cook!

Anyway, list in hand, PayTM in phone, I rushed out of the house to accomplish my duty.

I go to the local *tela-walla* (push-cart) for the greens.

I said: "*Bhaiyya*, 1 bunch of coriander."

Without blinking an eye, he points to a bunch of leaves at the far right end of his cart.

What if he's lying? How can I be sure he's telling the truth?

This is the part I hate. I don't know what coriander looks like!

But I have Google Baba.

"Ok Google, show me pictures of Coriander."

"Did you mean - Cilantro?" asks Google Baba.

"*Abe nahi*, Coriander...CORIANDER." I said loudly.

"Did you mean - Chinese Parsley?" asks Google Baba once more.

"I know I should have taken a Microsoft phone, dammit."

I put my trust in the tela-walla, and take the greens.

Next up in the list: Banana.

I know many of you would be smirking at my naivety saying- "What's the big deal in buying Bananas, ha ha ha", but did you know there are 2 varieties of bananas?

There's the *Yelaki*, the extremely sweet, smaller variety and there's the larger banana called the *Robusta*.

The most obvious question to be asking while buying a banana is:

"When do you want to eat it?"

If you want to eat it immediately, buy the bright yellow one, with some black spots. But if you want to have your banana a few days later, buy the greenish-yellow, unripe one.

The best part is: I didn't know any of this.

"Ok Google, how to select a Banana?"

"Choose bananas with slight green on stem and tip. Store unripe bananas at room temperature. Store ripe bananas for up to two weeks in the refrigerator."

"Hmm....." I pondered over this new piece of information for a while.

"So Bangalore's average temperature during summer is 35 degrees, which is 10 degrees above room temperature, and assuming the ripening will take 2 minutes instead of 2 weeks due to pesticides, global warming, inflation, Dhinchak Pooja etc......."

"I'll take the ripe one. *Robusta* let's go."

I got the other essentials pretty easily.

The last part: Urad Dal and Towar Dal.

I eat dal very well. Dal Makhani, Dal Tadka, Plain Dal, Dal diluted with 90% water.....anything.

But I have had no clue on which dal I had been eating all this while.

"Ok Google, show me pictures of Urad Dal."

Google Baba shows me a picture of a masala dosa and a vada.

"Google! I'm not ordering food from my college canteen!" I exclaimed.

As many of you *don't* know, Urad dal is a white, flat grain used to make dosa batter. And Towar Dal is a yellow, flat grain, also called as Pigeon Pea, used to make, well.........dal.

I've learnt a lesson from my experience while shopping for groceries.

....
....
....

I'm changing to a Microsoft phone.

Chapter 5

FINDING A GIRLFRIEND

In my honest opinion, it was easier to find a new five hundred rupee note during demonetization than finding a girlfriend today.

Girls, in general, expect a lot from guys. He should be tall, dark, sweet and comforting.

Sweet and Comforting?

Attention all Ladies: Do you want a boyfriend or a Cadbury Silk?

Guys don't have much of a problem while deliberating with choices. The only condition to be satisfied is that the girl must be a ….girl.

Always remember, 5 out of 4 girls will reject you on the first proposal!

Some guys have it easy. They have a suave way of conversing which automatically ensures that their number is stored in every girl's contact list.

I was talking to my friend outside the class the other day when:

"Hi Anjali!" he waved to a girl passing by.

"Who's that? Sister?" I asked.

"No bro, that's my schoolmate." he answered.

Another girl passed us.

"Hi Shwetha!" he said.

"Now, who is this?" I asked once again.

"She's my college mate."

And one more time, he waved to another girl. This time, timidly.

"Who's this? Your soul mate?" I concurred, coughing up a laugh.

He started to cry. "No bro, CHECKMATE."

Of course, not every boy has Lady Luck riding alongside him.

Academically inclined persons usually invent pickup lines they get from their tuition classes.

"You look $1/\cos C$ today," my classmate told a girl.

"Excuse me?" she stared at him.

"Heh heh, according to Trigonometric rules and the sides of a right triangle, $1/\cos C = \sec C$. Therefore, you look sexy today." He grinned, expecting a hug and a kiss.

She slapped him.

Moral of the story:

Trigonometry is injurious to health.

Chapter 6

PICKUP LINES

For today's generation, being in a relationship is a feat in itself.

"I cleared JEE with an All India Rank of 5," one boy said.

"I have 5 girlfriends," another said.

"Guruji, please teach me," the IIT boy said.

In this age and time of Whatsapp and Facebook, communication is not a problem.

Romance is.

If you want to research about your potential girlfriend, log onto Facebook or Instagram and you are set to go.

Pickup lines are supposed to charm a girl and sweep her off her feet.

But with me being ME, I tried a different approach.

I messaged a girl:

"Roses are Red,"
"Violets are Blue,"

"This is a love message,"
"How may I help you?" I typed.

She blocked me on Whatsapp.

Next, I tried a mathematical approach.

"If you are $\sin^2\theta$, then I am $\cos^2\theta$: together we will be one."

"I hate Maths," she said, and walked away.

But I would not give up.

"Are you trash?" I asked.

She looked at me with a perplexed expression.

"Because I would LOVE to take you out." I ended.

"What is this?" she gestured at her hand.

"Your *chappal* (slipper)," I replied, confused.

"What are *chappals* used for?" she said menacingly.

I got the message.

***

I had to try, one last time.

I unfriended my friend on Facebook suggesting these silly pickup lines he procured from his college Whatsapp group, who again got it from Facebook.

"Nice profile picture," I messaged her.

"Thank You," she messaged back.

"The flower in the picture looks really beautiful." I messaged.

A few tense moments passed. No reply from her side.

She had to reply now, fast. My data pack was getting over.

"And what about me?" she typed.

I smiled.

The fish had taken the bait. Did I mention she was Bengali?

I typed, albeit slowly.

"I was talking about you."

Silence.

And almost immediately:

"Awww….that's really sweet of you. Thank you so much! (Blushing smiley)"

"OMG that was very original!" she messaged.

"So……."

"Yes?" I replied.

"Want to go out for a coffee?"

Ladies and Gentlemen, that's how it's done.

Chapter 7

COMPLIMENTING A GIRL

Macha, I have a problem.

I don't know how to compliment a girl.

So the other day, my cousins and I were chilling in my uncle's house, when:

"Hey everyone!" my aunt, who had just returned from the US, walked in.

I hid the Pepsi bottle under the pillow. I was now sitting on the Pepsi bottle.

"Hi!" we all screamed at the same time.

"Guess who's on the line?"

"Hrithik Roshan?" I shouted.

My aunt gave me a deadpan expression. "It's Shruti!"

The Pepsi bottle broke and started to overflow. I was on a diet since 2 weeks; still how it broke I don't know.

Shruti was my cousin from the US, and my aunt's daughter. The last time she was in India was two years ago.

It was a video call, so all of us were forced to make a nice expression.

"Hiiiiiii!" Shwetha screamed. Shwetha was my uncle's daughter. She screamed so loudly that the neighbour's dog started barking.

"Hello Shruti!" said my older brother.

'Hi','hello','how are you'- these are the most boring words on the planet to greet someone you know very well.

Cousins are like good friends. Shruti was exactly my age, and hence we shared a good rapport.

"Oh wait! Lemme check my makeup," I could hear her say over the phone.

Finally, the phone came to me.

"Hi Shivaaa!!" she smiled.

"You've become fat." I said.

Her smile vanished.

Suddenly, everyone in the room become silent. The silence was eerie and profound. No one had a pin to check how silent the room was, but you get the idea. A few seconds later, my uncle and brother started howling with laughter. My cousin sister gave me a dirty look.

My aunt from the US looked at me in horror.

"How could you say something like that?!!" she exclaimed.

"What? She's become fat; put on weight to be precise. She could use some exercise. That's my observation, I'm an engineer. What's wrong?" I rallied my defence.

"You better make it up to her!" my aunt said menacingly.

"Hey! It was a joke! Everyone was being extremely boring by saying hi, hello; I thought I'd say something different!"

"Dude, you never tell a girl that she's put on weight," Shwetha interjected. "It's the number one unwritten rule."

"I studied CBSE. They never taught us all this."

Look, I was joking with her, and nothing else. Good friends can take a joke, right?

But in retrospect, she did look like she had been avoiding the fruits and vegetables.

"Shruti's really upset. She was crying on the phone," my aunt informed me.

"Do you want tissue," I asked insensitively.

"No silly, listen. Say sorry, and apologize."

A funny thing happened just then. Immediately after saying the word "apologize", she started laughing and walked away, shaking her head all the while.

I wonder why.

***

Later in the day, my phone pinged. It was a Whatsapp message from Shruti.

"I'm not sure in what world saying – 'you've become fat' is an appropriate greeting to your cousin you haven't seen in two years, but it's nice to see that you've developed manners since we last spoke."

"Hope you're doing well too."

Ok, let me play it cool.

"Hey, ok I'm sorry! Everyone was saying such nice things.....don't take it seriously!" I messaged Shruti back.

"Or should I have said you have become thin." I added.

No response that day.

Maybe bad network.

***

The next day, I get a reply back.

"Let me know when you learn to make a good joke, then I'll bother to take it as such." Shruti had messaged.

Wow, if this message was any more acidic, I'd have to call it vinegar.

I lost my temper.

"Shruti calm down, it was a joke."

"You're not fat."

"I heard you're working out! I am too! Both of us need to lose the pounds."

I regretted my actions immediately.

3 minutes later:

Me : "Sorry sorry"
: "Sorrreeeeyyy"
: "srrrrryyy"
: "SORRY"

I tried calling her on Whatsapp (because India-US calls can clean up your bank account).

Shruti : "Sorry can't talk now. What's Up?"
Me : "Are you still mad?"

Blue tick, yet no response.

Now I know why my aunt started laughing when she said 'apologize'.

I was narrating this incident to my Dad. He elicited the same response as my uncle and brother.

"Tell her there is no one as beautiful as her. She'll fall for it."

"Dad, what advice is this?"

"I know women. Just tell her that." My dad was very sure.

"That's what you think." My mom said from the hallway.

"Appreciate women, and they will forgive all your mistakes. I have used this tactic for years."

"EXCUSE ME?" my mom glared.

"What? What did I say wrong?"

"You can't say things like that," my mom walked away angrily.

Now my Mom and Dad started fighting.

I walked up to my dad and said: "Dad, better to apologize to Mom. Appreciate her, she will forgive you."

Appreciating a girl is like opening a Pandora's box.

Damned if you do, Damned if you don't.

Chapter 8

MASS BUNK: THE POWER OF AN IDEA

An idea.

Leading to whispers.

Leading to action.

Ideas have been credited with the rise and fall of empires, with the start of something new, or even the inception of a glorious future.

But, can an idea: translate into a mass bunk?

Let's find out.

It was a normal day at college. The Physics lecturer was droning on about atoms and how excited they can get. Clearly, the excitement was not translating down to the classroom.

I was sitting in the last bench, with my mouth wide open. I was just a minute away from drifting into deep sleep. I was bowling to Sachin, with Dhoni keeping the wickets and Virat Kohli umpiring. I was going to bowl the Ball of the Century when:

"*Aila*, I have an idea." Sachin said.

"Sachin Sir? But I have not bowled yet," I replied.

"Get up!" Sachin grabbed me by the shoulders and started shaking me.

"Manhandling! Virat Sir please help," I pleaded to the umpire.

Sachin slapped me twice.

"Howzzat!" I appealed.

Virat Kohli held up the finger.

"Wake up!!!" my friend jerked me awake.

"Sachin! Virat! Dhoni! Autograph I need," I mumbled, clearly in a daze.

Rohan, my best friend, and my bench mate, tried to shake me awake.

"Dude, Swamy Sir has been looking at you since the last 15 minutes; you're going to get thrown out of class."

"Hmm……ok sorry," I said. "Let's concentrate now."

Hardly ten minutes had passed when Rohan elbowed me.

"Psst….Shiva listen."

"Hmmm….what dude."

"Dude, let's bunk the next class."

I was shocked. I did not expect this from Rohan.

I expected him to bunk the entire day. Only one class? This was very disappointing from his side.

I didn't argue. "Ok," I said.

I whispered to the person sitting in front of me. "Bro, Rohan and I are bunking the next class. Give proxy for us."

He was texting his girlfriend.

"Hi Baby, sorry..........I miss you too! Next class is a mass bunk, I'll meet you at the canteen(smiley face)." the message read.

He gave me a thumbs up.

I never said it was a mass bunk, I had said that Rohan and I were bunking the next class.

The rules of the game had changed.

***

Readers, there are a few fundamental rules for every mass bunk to become a success.

Rule 1: No one should know who started the mass bunk.

Rule 2: Thou shall not stay in class if there is a mass bunk.

Rule 3: The Class Representative (CR) should be the last to know about a mass bunk. It is up to him/her to face the heat from the lecturer's side. After all, the CR is the face of the class. Our class cannot lose face at any cost.

Rule 4: Students with low attendance will be exempted from a mass bunk, only under special circumstances and with written permission from the class clown.

I have to say, Rule 2 is the most crucial during any mass bunk.

If the teacher enters the class, and not a single soul is present, no one in the class loses attendance.

But even if one person decides to attend the next class, the entire class loses attendance; except yours truly.

Obviously, a lot of cajoling went into coaxing the class topper to support the mass bunk. I felt like I was the Quit India Movement and the class topper the British.

"Girish, listen. We're planning a mass bunk in the next period. Don't attend the next class." I whispered.

"*Dei*! No no no! Not at all! Mass bunk is a sin! You will get punished for this. You will go to hell!"

I decided to play it safe.

"Bro- ok, let's compromise. If you support the mass bunk now, I will treat you at the canteen."

Girish had a weakness. If something was free, he couldn't refuse.

"Hmm…….treat….hmmm,"

"Anything you like," he was going to say yes.

"Ok……but I need a Black Forest pastry, with extra chocolate sauce."

I did the math. I felt like slapping Girish. A Black Forest Pastry was Rs.60, extra chocolate sauce was Rs.10. That made the total bill to 70 bucks.

I would make Rohan pay the bill.

"Ok, done! Do we have a deal? Will you bunk the next class?" I needed a confirmation.

"Sure...anything for Black Forest!" he smirked.

By this time, everyone had figured out that something was going on in class. Nobody knew what, but they knew something was going on. The news of a mass bunk started to travel from the last bench, where Rohan and I were seated, to the outskirts of the first bench.

No Whatsapp messages were used – by pure word of mouth (and 70 rupees), mass bunk fever had suddenly spread like wildfire and everyone in the class started to make plans to waste the next 50 minutes.

I even wrote "MASS BUNK NEXT CLASS" in huge letters on a piece of paper and started waving it to the next row to get their attention.

Did I mention that a Physics Class was going on all this while?

Quantum Mechanics was suddenly pushed to the backburner.

***

The next period, no one came to class.

Hence, proved: a successful mass bunk.

An idea.

Leading to whispers.

Leading to action.

THE POWER OF AN IDEA.

Because once an idea has made its way into your head, you can never get it out, however hard you try.

You can only choose to either agree or disagree with the idea.

Or with yourself.

PART 3

KABHI LOGIC, KABHI HUM

Chapter 1

CHAOS IN THE KITCHEN

I got up in the morning and basked in the beautiful sunlight filtering into my room. I completed my morning rituals and stepped into the kitchen, expecting a delicious start to a beautiful day.

And then I remembered.

My mother was away for the morning. My brother had a college team cricket match. Thus, all the cooking fell on my father's shoulders. All hell was about to break loose.

My father was very eager to exhibit his culinary skills and stepped into the kitchen with numerous ideas up his sleeve. He asked me whether I wanted parathas or omelette for breakfast.

I replied that I was happy with a bowl of cereal and bread, which would reduce any complications and uncertainties associated with breakfast. My father wouldn't hear of such things and immediately set out to make a cheese omelette. That was the day when I promised myself that I would learn cooking; starting from boiling some milk.

My father cracked two eggs and started to whisk them in a glass bowl; all the while waving the stirrer around like a magic wand in the hands of a magician gone berserk, giving me an unceremonious taste of whipped egg. Butter to be applied to a pan took flight from the butter knife and planted itself on the adjacent wall as my father quarrelled with the tools of the kitchen in desperation. The scene before me gave thoughts on whether my father was cooking up a meal or cooking up a disaster. Grated cheese sprinkled itself on the kitchen floor as my father fumbled with the packet, all the while trying to multitask by cutting onions and putting chillies into the pan. My mind automatically started preparing itself for a direct lunch as breakfast suddenly seemed like a very distant dream. I excused myself and exited the kitchen with seemingly unforgettable memories.

I was in for a pleasant surprise when the omelette arrived at the dining table and contrary to my expectations, it was spectacular! I looked at my father with pride and started to praise his cooking skills. At that very moment, the doorbell rang and my mother entered. Just then, I remembered.

"Dad, have you cleaned the kitchen?"

Before my father could answer, my mother glided into the kitchen -

Another hell was about to break loose!

~~~ ~~~ ~~~

Chapter 2

TO JOG or NOT TO JOG?

In today's ever changing world, there are a lot of trends being set, be it by companies or people. People have been bitten by the technology bug, the work bug or some even by bed bugs. In my case, it was the fitness bug that got to me first.

I was dreaming of playing football in space when the alarm interrupted my goal. It rang sharply, forcing me to get out my slumber. I switched off the alarm, and again went back to sleep. But the alarm was determined that I shouldn't score the match winning goal and rang again, this time even louder. I decided that it was better to give in to the alarm's demands.

I switched on the light and glanced at the clock groggily, the minute and hour hands shifting out of focus. As my eyes adjusted themselves to the sudden brightness, the time read – 5:30 am.

Excellent.

Early morning was a great time to exercise and fight the flab.

After a few stretching exercises, I set out. As soon as I got into the open grounds, a cold burst of air hit me in the face. I rubbed my palms together to keep myself warm, although I had a jacket on. Early morning was indeed beautiful, the fresh air floating through the atmosphere in the form of gentle breezes.

Well, time to start.

It was harder than I had expected. All the pizzas, sweets and Manchurians weighed me down as I stood gasping for breath after a mere 10 metres. But I willed myself to go on. As I was about to continue my jog, I noticed a boy of about my age holding a dog on a leash. The dog was pulling the boy around as it sniffed at every other bush and car tyre in the area. After a while, it stopped near a tree. To my surprise, the dog raised its leg and started to answer nature's call, quite loudly I must add. The owner instinctively looked up and gazed at the heavens above. I wanted to remind the owner that there were no meteor showers coming anytime soon and that the meteorological department had predicted a bright sunny day, but I remembered my manners.

I continued my jog for about 2 more minutes when I started panting again. Jogging and running always looks easy whenever Usain Bolt raced down the track at lightning speed. I did try that once, but discontinued after the neighbourhood aunties complained that they could not take their children out whenever I was running as they did not deem it "safe" and condemned my activities as "dangerous". I wondered if Bolt had to face similar problems.

It had been around 6:00 am when the Sun's rays blessed the Earth and people started to come out of their houses for their daily exercise. What I witnessed took me by surprise. It was a fashion parade that came out on the road. Every second person was wearing a Nike, Reebok or Adidas apparel. It didn't look like anybody had the intention of burning some calories, but instead wanted to showcase their modelling skills. Bright neon shorts adorned the ramp (also known as road) ,as men had bands around their heads and a water bottle in their hand. As my throat was dry, I stopped and asked one of the men for some water. He replied:

"Sorry, I only consume energy drinks." He smiled and continued his walk.

Well yes, he had a point.

A fancier name for *lassi* could be "energy drink".

On the last leg of my jog, I started to notice the type of walkers. One man, in his early thirties, was walking down the path briskly as if he were late for a meeting. Another woman, in her late 40's, was leisurely taking a walk down the garden lane and breathing in the fresh morning air. Suddenly, out of the blue, an enthusiastic cyclist burst onto the footpath, speakers blaring some metal band's song. I believe the metal band in question has something to do with a chemical element and a maiden. The two walkers, initially focused on their respective walks, whipped their head towards the cyclist and offered him a piece of their minds.

I decided that I had had enough exercise for one day and headed to the nearest restaurant, ordering a butter dosa. The satisfaction one gets after a rigorous workout; and it gets even better when you order your favourite item to gorge on …………..is just bliss. It can't be described, but needs to be experienced.

Some people might complain:

"Didn't you just go for a run? How will you lose weight if you keep eating like this"?

To them I say:

"Life is all about living in the present. Right now, the present for me is this spicy dosa and not your bitter comments."

Thus everyone lived happily ever after.

Chapter 3

BAS KARO TRAFFIC!

My father drove the car towards Pai Viceroy, one of Bangalore's finest restaurants. My brother and I were warming the back seat of the car, while my mother occupied the front seat. I was busy messaging my friend a joke while my brother was looking out of the window, making a visual map of all the streets in Bangalore inside his head. Our monthly outing was long due, and had been postponed due to my first terminal exams. It really was a funny thing though. Whenever I had exams, my brother would be having fun. Whenever his exams started, I would be having fun. So either way, one of us always used to get a dose from our parents when the other was studying.

Anyway, we had started from home quite early. It was a weekend, so we knew that the traffic situation would be crazy. Half the signals wouldn't be working, so the chaos would be exponential. My father tried to use the shortcut, which was through narrow lanes, but was cut short by some construction board which said

– "MIND YOUR HEAD". Cars couldn't go through, but all the motorists took off their helmets, bent down, "MINDED THEIR HEADS", and rode off into the dust and smoke. So we had to take the main road.

The main road was even worse. There were cars, buses, bikes, trucks and anything with wheels all over the place. There was a traffic policeman, only one at the centre of a major turning. He had no clue what was going on and kept on waving his hand up and down, right and left like a drill master, so that all vehicles could keep going whenever and wherever they wanted to. We had a table reservation at 7pm, and it was now 6:30pm. I anticipated that the way things were going, we wouldn't be there on time, and hence started looking out for other restaurants nearby.

Just then, we took a turning. About 100 metres in front of us, was a traffic signal, with a big green signboard screaming – 15 seconds. My father suddenly changed gears and the car started to gain speed.

90 metres, 75 metres, 50 metres, 15 metres …………………..just 1 second left.

We were just about to cross the white line when the traffic signal turned red, and the signboard displayed a countdown of 125 seconds.

My father slammed the brakes. He grunted in frustration. "We won't be there on time." he declared.

125 long seconds went past.

Finally, the long wait was over and we were off.

A biker was trying to overtake us. A lady was riding pillion with him. Unnecessarily, he kept braking on the way so that she would keep falling on him. Somewhere down the line, I feel *Bollywood* has spoilt us.

I think that day Lady Luck decided she needed a vacation, as we got stuck at another traffic signal. Beggars started to swarm the cars at the traffic junction and began knocking on the car windows.

One man in a red car gave the beggar Rs.100.

"Hello, give me 90 rupees change," he snarled at the beggar.

"Sir, I don't have change. Shall I transfer it through PayTM?" the beggar replied.

We reached the hotel 30 minutes late and surprisingly, our reservation was still intact. I was so famished that I could eat a horse.

Which brings me to a very important question: Why does anyone eat a horse?

We were halfway through our dinner when the lights went out in the restaurant.

Lady Luck was definitely on vacation.

Chapter 4

GOOGLE MAPS, WHERE ARE YOU?

We had just left for Sringeri, a hill station in Karnataka. Sringeri is a beautiful place with great historical importance, and is the abode of the Sringeri Sharada Mutt, established by Adi Shankara, a Hindu saint. We decided to drive down and thus embarked on our long drive into the mountains.

It all began one fine day-when I was drooling on the bed.

I was in 12th at that time, and had just finished my Board exams a month ago. Usually when exams are done, students tend to celebrate. But today, I had to force myself out of bed to study for engineering entrance exams.

"Life is an ongoing process, and one must adapt to its changes", a great person had once said.

I would love to ask this great person if he has ever given a CBSE exam.

My mother was complaining on the number of entrance exams I was writing, and how it had ruined our holiday plans. Our Sringeri trip was scheduled on 20th and 21st of April, while I had exams on 18th and 19th.

Today was the 16th.

As usual, I was roaming around the house from one room to other (anything to avoid studying) - reading the paper, cleaning my cupboard, helping my mother in the kitchen, avoiding my father after breakfast (that's when he's most angry) etc etc. Why are fathers always angry?

The time was now 9 in the morning.

Suddenly, my mother said: "Why don't we leave for Sringeri today?" she asked us.

"When?" I asked.

"Now." she said.

"NOW?" we all shouted. "How can we leave now? We haven't planned anything" I said.

"That's fine. You and your elder brother never plan anything anyway." she replied slyly.

I hung my head in shame.

"Also," she added, "if we leave now, we can reach there by nightfall, finish the darshan and drive back the next day."

"Sounds reasonable," my father seconded it.

"Okay, so everyone has 1 hour. Pack whatever you need, and by 10am, we should all be in the car." My mother gave her orders.

After that, it was a mad scramble for things. We literally threw our clothes into the bags and rushed out of the house. Hopefully the fan, geyser, iron box and switches were all off. Else God help us.

For every trip, the one thing you should never leave your house without, is Google Maps. This is by far one of the best inventions I have ever come across, which has helped innumerable number of people around the world to find their way to a place, solely relying on the tiny blue arrow for navigation.

But today would be the first time that we would be using the voice activation feature in Maps. My mother was navigating and my father was driving, while my brother and I were stretching ourselves in the back seat. My mother typed in *Neelamangala*, our first destination.

This is what we heard.

"Bangal-ore to Neel-maan-gyala, 26 km."

"Neel what?" I asked.

A British lady was giving us directions and *Neelamangala* almost sounded like some new dish.

Nevertheless, we reached our destination without any hassles.

"Type in Chikmagalur," my father said.

"Neel-maan-gyala to Chik-maag-loor, 219 km."

"We should have gone by bus. Much better than this," my brother muttered.

"You would go walking if you had a choice," I retorted.

He grinned at me.

As we were going on the National Highway road, a Tata Sumo zoomed past us at top speed and swerved madly at a turning. My father was furious. He accelerated and finally we were just behind the Sumo. On the back of the Sumo was written –"For Rash Driving, Please call 978*******."

My father gave me his phone and said-

"Call this number and tell them about this fool of a driver."

I obediently called the number. I could hear the ringtone.

"*Dhoom Machale, Dhoom Machale, Dhoom, Dhoom......*"

"Hallo?"

"Sir, does the car KA 45 ** **** belong to you?"

"Ya."

"Sir, your driver is driving extremely rashly. Please reprimand him."

"*Oi* hello boss, I am only the driver. This is my number. I am not driving rashly. It's okay only." With that he cut the call.

As we were approaching our destination, the sky started to darken. It was a mountainous region and we definitely needed to go slow. We once again, used Google Maps. It mapped out a complicated route with even more complicated directions. So we decided to ask someone. We saw a villager walking along the road.

"Sir, how to go to Sringeri?"

"*Onde rodu sir, straightaa hogi* (one single road, keep going straight)," he said happily.

"Ok thank you," I waved.

Maps were showing us an alternate route which had atleast 10 turns. We decided to go for the former.

As soon as we took the route given by the villager, suddenly the British lady spoke:

"GPS Signal lost."

Chapter 5

THE LOVE FOR FOOD or LOVE AND FOOD?

You know those movies in which the hero and the heroine are at the marriage hall, smiling at each other(mostly after the hero has had a word with the baddies) and in the final scene, both look at the camera, where the movie ends and the director's name pops up on the screen. You leave the hall, satisfied that you had got your money's worth and a happy ending.

It's the same thing in all movies. Boy meets girl, girl meets boy, both fall in love, a fight for justice ensues, and a dance in Switzerland later, they get married. You would say:

"How does that matter? Every love story has a happy ending".

But here's the catch.

It's been six months since the boy and girl have been married. They've been working, chatting and enjoying each other's company. They eat out everyday too. Suddenly, the boy realizes that he misses his mother's special "*dal chawal*" (Dal Rice) and asks his wife to make it. He says with enthusiasm:

"Honey, we've been eating out for quite some time now."

"Ya babe. So?" she replies.

"And....you know I love *Dal Chawal*, right? I order it wherever we go!"

Could you please make my favourite *dal chawal*?"

The wife looks at him with a bewildered expression.

"Dal chawal? Babe, isn't that a Lebanese dish?"

In today's world, cooking has become a premium. The attitude of "Let's order" has taken over the minds of the present generation and people are quickly moving towards the "grab a bite" segment. Traditional cooking has taken a backseat in the wave of cookery shows, where most of the time secrets are hidden from the viewer. Baking cakes and pastries have become quite the fad, with every Tom, Dick and Harry saying – "I can bake!" But if you ask them - "Can you cook?" they reluctantly change topic.

We keep forgetting that we're Indian. Food comes first in our priority list. Indian food has everything. Tangy, spicy, sour, sweet – we have all flavours in check and in the right proportion. Every time we meet up – be it a casual meeting, a business meeting or a marriage function, food is our top priority. When people go to a marriage, the deciding factor is not how big the hall is or how expensive the bride's jewellery was. It all boils down to how good the food was.

Since we Indians love good food, why do we have to compromise on our culture? Are we too lazy or too cynical? Of course, today's youngsters (including me) are more into gadgets and stuff like "*Jeena hai tho padna hai*" (If you want to live, you have to study) as compared to learning to cook. But when they go abroad to study, they keep lamenting over the phone on how much they miss their "*maa ki daal*" and Mom's beautifully hand crafted gulab jamun, swimming in the hot, lip smacking sugar syrup.

Well, that's the bottom line for Indian cooking.

Take over the legacy. It's your time.

I bet Sanjeev Kapoor is smiling to himself right now.

Note for my foreign friends:

Sanjeev Kapoor is a famous celebrity chef from India. He is the best.

Chapter 6

WHAT'S YOUR NAME AGAIN?

Have you ever been in a position where you meet your long lost friend, but you've forgotten his name?

It happened to me.

I was going to cross the road when:

"Oi! Dude!" I waved madly to a boy on the other side of the road.

"Oh hi!" he waved back. I went to his side of the road.

"Whats up da? Long time it's been!" I said.

"Yeah bro, time just flies. What are you doing nowadays?"

"Studying mostly. How about you?"

He smiled. "College is chilled bro. We study for exams only at the last minute. It's fun."

We walked for about a kilometre when it hit me.

I had forgotten his name.

Aha, but I had a better tactic.

"Bro, is your dad's name Gupta?" I asked him.

"Nope, it's Mehta." he replied innocently.

"*Acchha*...what's your full name?"

"Abhilash Mehta."

"Oh ok....your dad's name sounded familiar so I asked."

Haha, he never got to know.

As our conversation progressed, somehow it pricked me that I hadn't known his name before hand and confessed.

"Bro I had forgotten your full name so I tried to fool you and all. It's cool right?"

He started laughing.

"Dude,even I had forgotten your name and was going to ask you 5 minutes later."

Now I was going to punch him.

Chapter 7

BRO, WHERE'S THE TREAT?

Every time our friend's birthday comes up-
"Bro, treat bro."
He/She was born on that day, and for that we have to get a treat.
What logic is involved here?
Then starts the war of deciding where to go.
"Bro, Mcdee da. Sooper shakes they have."
Someone else quips - "Dude, Pizza Hut is better."
"*Nahi yaar*, Barbeque Nation. More variety."
Another friend says - "Dude, let's go to Anand Sagar."
Everyone stares at him like he had just murdered someone.

Why does this happen? If you ask today's generation, they will say that McDonald's or Pizza Hut is "cooler" than Anand Sagar or any other roadside restaurant.

I was curious. How is the "coolness quotient" of a restaurant measured? Is it by the number of Air Conditioners they have?

"Eh bro, what a PJ(Poor Joke)."

"Its class bro. Mcdee has class. Burgers have class. Dosa is like ok-ok."

Someone else chips in - "It's the pricing da. If you pay high, it must be good."

"But it's just potato in a bun," I said.

My friend got irritated. "Dude, if you give a treat in a high class place, your reputation is secured. It's important bro."

So the dosa takes the hit for reputation.

The thing is, we do so much for our friends. Be it from impressing them with the best of our clothes or taking them to the most lavish of restaurants. Then why is that after everyone leaves, we go and devour mom's homemade food?

Think about it. Can you eat pizza for an entire month? I doubt it. You will start salivating the moment you see a bowl of hot *gajar halwa.*(carrot halwa)

Or a Mysore Pak.

Or even a chum-chum.

Chapter 8

ECONOMICS: A DUMMIES GUIDE

If you are in an Economics classroom and everything the teacher is saying is going over your head (if you're sleeping in class), here's a quick guide on how to judge whether the economy of the country is doing well or not:

If the economy is doing well:

1. Neighbourhood aunties fighting with vegetable vendors reduce.
2. You get extra sambar for masala dosa.
3. Traffic policemen bribes reduce.
4. Less begging for pocket money with Mummy Papa.
5. Air hostess smiles extra in flights.
6. Teachers give more games periods.

If the economy is bad:

1. This parameter can be used by anyone, anywhere. Check the tummy size of your local politician.

If it's increasing: Economy is down.
If it's decreasing: Economy is up.

2. Aunties argue more. Hence noise pollution increases.
3. Sambar is replaced by water.
4. Discus throwers start using idlys in the Olympics.
5. Visits to Dominoes are replaced by visits to the local vada pav store.
6. Your coffee will start to taste salty.

In conclusion, the government must take immediate measures to:

1. Improve the Economy
2. Reduce Noise Pollution
3. And most importantly, save the prestige of sambar.

Hoping for the best :)

Chapter 9

MANAGEMENT LESSONS FROM WIFE

My mother was reading a book one fine Sunday morning. I casually glanced at the title.

"Learning Management skills from your Wife," the title ran.

I was perplexed.

"Mom, aren't you the Wife? Dad should be reading this book instead," I said.

My mother looked at me with a bored expression.

"I wanted to check if the author has written the book correctly."

~~~ ~~~ ~~~

Chapter 10

NORTH INDIANS Vs SOUTH INDIANS

This eternal debate has never ended, and never will.

Who is better? A South Indian? Or a North Indian?

"Bhai, North is the best, debate *katam*," Piyush, a Northie, said.

"Why bro? What do you have that we don't?" I asked him, the South Indian in me gearing up for a fight.

"What do we have? Alright let's go!"

"Honey Singh, Navjot Singh, Singh is King, Manmohan Singh"

"Pav Bhaji, Chicken Tikka, Aloo Paratha and Chola Batura"

"Virat Kohli, Bhajji, Sehwag and Sachin Paaji"

"Bro, Maharashtra is not North India," I said.

"Adjust karlo,"

"Peda, Jalebi, Gulab Jamun and even *Machli*" Piyush continued.

"Dude! Fish is famous in East India....I mean West Bengal!" I protested.

"Oi! Is Bengal in South India?" he asked.

"No…" I answered.

"Then it's included in North India," he shut me up.

"Punjabi, Sindhi, Gujarati, Bihari –all one family"

"You haven't seen DDLJ? What a tragedy!"

"Bollywood, Badshah, Bread Pakora are all from the North,"

"Stop cooking rice, because too many cooks spoil the broth!"

"It's time you learnt Hindi, its better you learn,"

"I don't mean to get political, but it's now AAP ka turn."

Mike drop.

I had had enough.

I started:

"Idly, Vada, Dosa - with extra Chutney"

"That's what you get when you try to act funny!"

"Tamil Nadu, Andhra, Karnataka and the Gulf"

"Don't try to mess around, or we'll beat you to pulp!"

"Rajni, Rajkumar, NTR, and Mammootty"

"We're so good at math and filter coffee!"

"Lungi Dance? You should try Chennai Express,"

"I mean the actual train, not the one that depressed!"

"IIT Delhi? How about IIT Madras?"

"At least then you might learn to have some class!"

"It's the end of the debate; I'm running out of rhymes!"

"*Ja chai leke aa*, with some extra lemon and thyme!"

I think I won this debate. What do you think?

Chapter 11

MAID IN INDIA

Raise your hands if you believe that Maid in India is much more important than Made in India.

It's true!

I remember the day our family moved into our new flat. I said:

"I am a strong, free willed and independent person. I will do the house cleaning myself."

After one day of dusting, doing the dishes, mopping the floor and finishing the laundry, I said:

"Hello Rekha aunty? I'm calling from D-101: can I please have your maid's number? We've just moved in, so I need someone to help with the cleaning. Thank you!"

Now, hiring a maid is not an easy matter. HR interviews are essential, but not necessary.

"Name?" my mom asked.

"Savitri," the maid said.

"Where do you live?"

"MK Road."

"Past work experience?"

"Uhh…..I've worked as a senior hygiene expert at my former employer's place, and was a sanitation supervisor at Green City Apartments."

"Give me a SWOT Analysis," my mom said.

"What?"

"SWOT! Strengths, Weaknesses, Opportunities and Threats."

"Hmm…" the maid mused.

"STRENGTHS: I can finish house cleaning within an hour."

"So fast??!" my mom exclaimed.

"I deliver quality and quantity Ma'am."

"WEAKNESSES: I do not accept second hand saris or shirts."

"OPPORTUNITIES: Festivals like Diwali, Christmas etc; extra payment can be expected."

"THREATS: Extremely small notice period given by employer while firing."

"Where do you see yourself in 5 years time?" my mom asked.

"In 5 years time……….?" Savitri mused.

"Yes, 5 years."

"Your house?" she answered cheekily.

"Ok. We will be giving you Rs.2000 per month. Come in the morning at 7 am, clean the house, do the dusting and wash the dishes. Deal?"

"No madam, please pay me Rs.2500 per month." Savitri said.

"Why? You do the same job in Rekha aunty's house, she pays you 2000 only!"

"Madam, nowadays prices are increasing, the IT sector is not doing well, the rupee is again sliding against the dollar, Sensex…."

" Ok, fine! Let's compromise. Rs.2200." my mom started to negotiate.

"No madam – 2300."

"2250." My mom persisted.

"2249," Savitri said.

"Done. You may join from tomorrow."

It is said that the head of the family is the father, and the head of the house is the mother.

But if the maid does not come for one day……

The heavens fall on our heads.

One fine day, I got up late as usual. I went to the kitchen. My mother was screaming over the phone hysterically.

"Savitri! You have not come for 6 days! The house is in a mess! You should have arranged for someone else to come in your place!"

"Madam I have gone to my native place – my mother's brother's sister's cousin's uncle's daughter's son's wedding is there, so I could not come." Savitri replied over the speaker phone.

"When will you be back??" my mother said, still fuming.

"One month madam," Savitri replied.

"WHAT?? No chance, you need not come here hereafter. I wish you all the very best in your future endeavours."

"Ok fine! Have fun trying to find a new maid madam!" Savitri laughed, and cut the phone.

For a moment, there was pin drop silence.

"Mom, what's for breakfast?"

I should have shut my mouth.

I was assigned to clean the dishes that day and sweep the house.

That night, I was dreaming about playing in the Indian Cricket Team. The cool drinks bottle during the drinks break looked like the green dishwashing liquid and my bat was a broom.

The Government supports 'Made In India.'

I support Maid in India.

Chapter 12

KEEP THE CHANGE: THE ONE RUPEE REVOLUTION

"Keep the Change."

Said no Indian ever.

We've all heard this at one point in our lives, right?

With American movies and shows taking the Indian Market by storm, a few catchphrases are definitely making the rounds among the country's youth.

"I'll be back." said my friend to me one day.

"Yeah, yeah – no issues. Take your time." I responded.

He had expected me to give an amazed or intimidated look.

"I'll be BACK." He tried again.

"*Arre ok baba*, you're going to the toilet right? Class doesn't start for another 10 minutes. Take your time."

Or how about another time:

"*How ya doin*?!" Rahul jumped out of nowhere in front of me, with a stupid grin on his face.

"Thanks man, I am fine."

"The Lannisters send their regards." he said solemnly.

"*Tera baap* send his regards, stop this catchphrase nonsense or I'll your tell your dad you're going out with Neha."

Both these guys have blocked me on Whatsapp.

Coming back to point:

We've been influenced so much by American culture that it sometimes filters down into our daily lives.

My friend and I had recently been to Café Coffee Day. I ordered a Café Mocha, while he ordered a Café Frappe.

As we kept chatting, I realized that both my time and coffee were over. I had to return home early for a family function.

I signalled to the waiter for the bill.

"Café Mocha- Rs.129, and Café Frappe – Rs 149." My friend read out. We paid our bills separately. I placed Rs.130 on the table, and asked for my one rupee change.

"GST included right?" I asked the waiter.

"Of course Sir."

My friend paid Rs.200 for his beverage, and told the waiter: "Keep the Change."

I was a bit confused at my friend's behaviour. The waiter was not. Who doesn't like a 51 rupee tip? Consequently, the waiter looked at me in disgust, returning my one rupee.

I kept it for him as a tip.

***

When we were outside the Coffee Day store, and out of the waiter's earshot, I screamed at my friend.

"What is WRONG with you?? What the hell does 'keep the change' mean?"

"Bro, calm down. It's the American Way. That's how we do things around here." he replied with an uncharacteristic swagger.

"Oh really? The other day, in the bus stand's public urinal – who was arguing with the guard? "I retorted.

2 DAYS BACK

"It says that the urinal is free! Why should I pay 2 rupees to you?" my friend had argued the other day in the bus stand. People started staring. Not at the urinal, at him.

"Sir, this is what my boss has told me to do. You have to pay Rs.2"

"No chance. This is how corruption builds up in this country. I won't pay."

"Sir, you will have to cough up 2 rupees. That's how we do things around here."

Almost immediately, a man came out of the public toilet, walked up to the guard and slammed a 10 rupee note on the desk.

"Keep the change," he said. He put on his sunglasses and walked away. Please note that this incident happened at 10 pm in the night.

"*Heh heh*, bro – you know me too well da. I was just trying to impress the two girls next to our seat! Anyway, you see American TV Shows? Over there for a cup of coffee, or a slice of pizza, the customers never collect back the change!"

"It gives you an ego boost, and elevates your status in society." My friend ended his monologue.

I wasn't convinced.

***

The very next day, I went to my local grocery store to buy a packet of bread.

"One bakery bread please," I said to the shopkeeper.

"That will be Rs.29," he said, as he placed the bread in my shopping cart.

I gave him Rs.30.

"Thank You," he said, and started attending to other customers.

I waited at the counter. The shopkeeper gave me a side glance, but continued to be absorbed in his own work.

Ten minutes passed. I had not budged from the counter. I was counting the number of Colgate brushes the shop had kept on display.

The shopkeeper figured out that he couldn't avoid me. He walked up to me.

"Yes Sir, do you want anything else?"

"No."

"Sir, then why are you waiting?"

"How much was my bakery bread?" I asked.

"Rs.29, Sir."

"How much did I give you?"

"Rs.30"

"So……………." I waited for him to get my drift.

"So…?" he genuinely looked confused.

"Where's my one rupee change?" I finally asked.

He looked at me for a full five seconds, without saying a word.

Suddenly, to my utter shock, he burst out laughing.

"Sir, what Sir…….you are asking for one rupee. You look well to do, and wouldn't bother much even if 100 rupees gets lost. One rupee? Really?"

"I want my money." I said adamantly.

"Ok sir, here's a chocolate." He smirked as he slid an Eclairs towards me.

"Are you trying to be funny? Give my coin now, or I'll come back later!" I erupted.

"Sir, I have to take care of the other customers. Please stop wasting my time." He started to move away from the counter.

"Wait." I held his arm.

I took a deep breath. And then:

"Let me tell you a story, a story of a rupee,"

"A quaint little coin, unlike Bappi Lahiri"

"A rupee in my pocket, is worth the change"

"When you go in a bus, you earn the conductor's praise!"

"Silly it may sound to argue over a coin,"

"But there are so many things you can buy, are you getting my point?"

"Matchbox, stamps, sometimes even candles"

"Without these things, life just dismantles!"

"Let's just say you sell 100 bakery bread loaves in a week. Each customer gives you Rs.30, but doesn't ask for the change."

"Which means, you've easily made a profit of Rs.100 a week, at any range."

"Wait, what if this is happening in 10 other shops?"

"Do the math! You're in for a shock!"

"It's easily a 1000 rupee profit a week – that's where corruption starts, feeding on the poor and the meek."

"Why stop at 10? Or 100? Let's make it a thousand shops across the country,"

"Adding more zeroes, it's a lakh of rupees! There goes your money, clearing the boundary,"

"It may seem like I'm wasting your time,"

"Yet, someone has to speak up for the coin and its shine."

"Then it's fine. I don't want my money."

"The least you can do, is give me a Coffee Bite with a little honey."

The customers were all dumbfounded. The shopkeeper's mouth was wide open.

"Excuse me, can you pass me the biscuit packet in front of you?" A man said from behind my back.

"Sure," I passed the packet to him.

"Thanks. Oh…..the price is Rs.19." he said, and paused.

Nobody moved in the shop. There was pin drop silence.

The atmosphere was tense.

"Here's Rs.20." the man said to the shopkeeper.

"Wait Sir, WAIT. Here's your one rupee." The shopkeeper frantically gave the man his coin.

"Keep the change." The man said, and walked away into the darkness.

~~~ ~~~ ~~~

Chapter 13

WRITING TO THE DEVIL

In the month of June 2017, my brother and I embarked on a journey to write an article on the Goods and Services Tax (GST), which was going to be implemented by the Government of India on July 1st, 2017.

It involved a lot of research, editing and drawing conclusions on certain topics based on our limited knowledge of the Indian tax system. We had put in about a week's worth of effort into this article, and finally at the end of 7 days, we had struck gold. Our finished product on GST was ready to be published.

Here is a little tip for all the budding writers out there: Whenever you send your article to a premier newspaper, DO NOT EXPECT them to reply with a mail saying:

"Congratulations, you are the first person in 10 years to send an article to us. We will be publishing your piece in tomorrow's edition."

It has never happened, and never will.

But we were amateurs! We had hoped for a red carpet welcome.

My brother and I were excited! This was the first time we had written an article together, and it may even get published! I imagined my name in the papers the next morning - suddenly my Facebook friend requests have gone through the roof, I start getting calls from relatives inviting me to their homes, NASA has announced that they will put me on Mars next Friday.

(because Friday is auspicious for South Indians)

A thrill went up my spine as soon as I hit the "SEND" button. I had sent our article to a leading daily.

My thoughts were interrupted by my father's voice:

"All that is ok, ask them when it will get published; and send another mail saying that if the article is going to be rejected, they should inform you about the same."

I scoffed at these comments. Who were they to reject us! It was not possible, I was sure of it. But I sent the mail with the additional comments anyway.

My father is a pragmatic man. Most of the time he's right about everything.

But if you're young and idiotic like my brother and I were, you don't listen to good, old "grey haired" advice.

ONE WEEK LATER

There had been no reply from the newspaper's side. Everything was going on as usual. My father was watching the news, my mother was complaining on how was Vijay Mallya's loan repayment details more important than drying the clothes (which I had conveniently forgotten to do), and my brother was being irritating.

Another day went by. Still no response from the newspaper's side. There were only 2 weeks to go for GST.

I had sent my mail to the editor of the paper. I had expected a reply from her thanking me for choosing their paper, and how honoured they would be to accept my article. I realized that I was starting to have very high expectations for impossible events.

I started making regular phone calls to the office of the newspaper.

"Hello, this is *** from *** Publications, how may I help you?"

"Hi Sir, this is Shiva Shankar, and I am calling from Bangalore. May I speak to Ms. Nikita, the editor?"

"*Madam nahi aaya hai. 2 pm ke baad call kijiye.*"(Madam has not arrived. Call after 2 pm)

"Ok thank you Sir. Jai Hind."

I called again after 2 pm.

"Hello"

"Hi Sir, this is Shiv......."

"Madam has not come to office. Call tomorrow."

This ritual of saying hello and getting information that "Madam" has not come to office went on for another week.

At this point, I went all guns blazing. I called the office again.

"Hellloo, how may…?"

"Boss, listen. I have been calling your office for the past one week, and every time I get a message saying that Madam has not come to office. You better…"

"Madam has not come. Call after 2 pm."

And he cut the call.

I looked at Baba Ramdev's Pranayama videos to calm down and ate some Patanjali biscuits. I started to think.

What if I withdraw my article from the paper? They don't know that I've sent them a gold mine! If an organization does not appreciate your efforts, you change the organization! I liked the idea.

But my mother was staunchly against this. "Wait for another 3 days and see. Nobody is waiting with a golden platter for your article. This is India: if you lose your place, 10 other people will be waiting to take it. Ok: leave all this now, and come for dinner."

"She's right," I thought to myself. My brother butted in – "Come for Dinner."

"Get Lost. Why am I following up with them so much? You should also do some work!"

He smirked. "I'm elder, so I make the younger sibling do all the work. That's how life works. You have a lot to learn, my child."

3 DAYS LATER

"Okay, I'm done waiting. I'm withdrawing the article effective immediately." I screamed at the wall clock in my room. It showed no expression.

My brother walked in.

"Shiva wait, today I will call up the newspaper's office, and talk to the editor. I'll see what I can do," he gave me an assuring pat on the shoulder.

I relaxed, took a deep breath, and acceded.

There's an old saying: There's always a lull before a storm.

2 HOURS LATER

I get a call from my brother.

"Hello Shiva, when did you send the article to the editor?"

"Oh that.....about two weeks back."

"Ok," and with that he cut the call.

"Hmm.........we will make a decision today," I thought to myself.

I finished my classes, went to the nearby bakery for tea, when suddenly my phone buzzed.

It was a text from my brother.

"Please call the editor on her personal line. This is her number."

That's it. No other explanation whatsoever. I was surprised and confused at the same time. What could have happened?

Brushing aside these speculations, I called up the editor's number.

"Hello," a stern voice replied on the other side.

"Hello Ma'am, my name is Shiva Shankar Iyer, and I am calling from Bangalore."

"Ok...." she heard me patiently.

"I had sent an article for publication in your newspaper about two weeks back, titled 'GST: Rise of the Indian Economy'......"

And that, Ladies and Gentlemen, is when the volcano erupted.

"Oh, so you are the co-author of the article? I have had someone call me five times today morning about the article, and he doesn't even know which email id the article has been sent to! What do you think about us? Why can't you co-ordinate with your co-author?" she screamed.

I could feel my phone getting warmer. I'm sure it was a battery problem.

"Ma'am but....." I tried to intervene.

"What BUT? WHAT BUT? We have over 53 articles on GST in the queue, and you think you are the only person writing about it?"

"Ma'am but I have mentioned in my mail that if you have rejected it, please send a mail back stating the same!" I interjected.

"Your article has not even been seen, so there is no question of accepting or rejecting it in the first place! You have the nerve to keep calling and bothering us with your repeated phone calls. If your article has been accepted, we will forward it to the relevant section. We do not send return mails for rejected articles. Until then, keep checking our paper, and do not call again."

Before I could say anything, she slammed the phone down.

It felt like a whirlwind had just passed by, and my head was spinning.

5 HOURS LATER

"And that was what happened! Now I have no idea on the status of our article." I exclaimed over the phone to my father.

"Ha ha ha! Good, good – now you know how the world works. Life is not so easy!"

Fathers are so typical. They keep trying to expose you to the big, bad world while keep mothers try to protect you from the big, bad world.

"Why don't you write an article about this? Send it to the same editor you spoke to! She might take it in good humour," my mother said over the speaker phone.

"Yes! Why not? That's a good idea!" My father seconded.

"Hmm....let me think about it......what about the title of the article?"

"Publishing in a newspaper?"

"Demerits of newspaper publishing?"

"Excuse me, what demerits, are we talking about demonetization? Conjure up a fancy name," my mother said.

"Well, she did shout like the devil," I thought out aloud.

"There you go," my father said.

Hence the title: "WRITING TO THE DEVIL."

EPILOGUE

"So Shiva, I heard you had got quite a dressing down from the editor. How about that? It could have been me!" my brother laughed.

"Only one person should have co-ordinated with the editor," I said with clenched teeth.

"*Arre* let bygones be bygones. I'm the elder brother, it is my responsibility to teach you about life and why I have more experience in dealing with such matters. You have a lot to learn." he smirked.

That day my brother turned a wiser man: He learnt how hard I can punch.

Chapter 14

RAKSHA BANDHAN

Traditionally every year, Raksha Bandhan is celebrated with pomp and fanfare. It is a festival which celebrates the bond between brothers and sisters. All squabbling and fighting has to be ceased for a day as brothers and sisters unite to tie *rakhis* and exchange gifts.

On this occasion, sisters tie a sacred thread called *rakhi* to their brother's wrists and brothers, in turn, promise that they would always protect their sisters.

That very morning, my friend Rohan came to the class in tears.

"Bro, are you ok? Were you cutting onions in the morning?" I asked.

His sobbing increased.

"Alright, sorry........tell me what happened."

He took a deep breath, and his whimpering reduced.

"You know about Neha right? The girl I keep telling you about?"

"Yep."

"She sent me a Whatsapp message. Here, see."

I grabbed his phone and had a look.

It read: "If I can choose someone in my next life, then I will choose you."

"Love You."

"Dude! This is fantastic! Why are you crying?" I bellowed.

"Idiot – scroll down." Rohan bellowed.

I scrolled down further.

"Brother." The message ended.

"Happy Raksha Bandhan."

I returned his phone.

"The text says that you are her brother in her next life. Not in this one! Congratulations!" I consoled him.

He gave me a pitiful look, and walked away cursing his bad fate for having such a useless friend like me.

My phone beeped. One notification.

"On this special day, I want to thank you from the bottom of my heart for being the best brother in the world! Happy Raksha Bandhan!"

Now I started wailing loudly.

"Hi bro! Were you cutting onions in the morning?" Karthik asked.

PART 4

TRAVEL DIARIES

Chapter 1

BUTTERING THE DOSA: A TRIP TO NORTH KARNATAKA

During the Christmas vacations, my family and I set out from Bangalore, the city of iPhones, set dosas and unpredictable traffic to the evergreen and serene lands of North Karnataka.

We set off early in the morning, sleepy, but in high spirits. The trip would be a rejuvenating change compared to our daily and monotonous routine, where students went to school, office goers went to office and the watchman was caught sleeping on a regular basis. A change once in a while would have been appreciated.

We stopped at Tumkur, where we had a delicious breakfast which consisted of *idly*, *vada* and piping hot coffee. The *chutney* in Tumkur was a tinge spicier than the one found in Bangalore, and its people definitely had wit faster than their public transport! It was a relief from the fast food restaurants in the Garden City. Chitradurga offered us refreshments after which we arrived at the most awaited part of our journey – Davangere.

We had heard praises for the Davangere "*Benne Dosa*" (Butter Dosa) and we were very eager to try it. As major foodies, we were excited to try the much hyped up dosa of Davangere.

The waiter seated us at a table and asked us what we would like to have. I immediately rattled off in broken Kannada that the waiter could take our order for 4 *Benne Dosas*. He scribbled the order in his pad and marched towards the kitchen. We waited in anticipation. Twenty minutes later, the waiter emerged from the kitchen with four *Benne dosas* whose aroma wafted across the hall and made our mouths water. As the waiter placed the dosas on the table, I could see the butter melting and slowly sliding down the dosas, effortlessly. It was like poetry in motion. All the praises for the dosas had not been in vain. We attacked the dosas without delay and at the end of ten minutes, we had gained immense satisfaction and a lot of calories.

To complete the meal, we wanted to order buttermilk. Davangere was a pure Kannada speaking place, with little room for English invasion. I had managed to convey the message of the dosas to the waiter with my limited knowledge of Kannada, but with the order for buttermilk I was truly stumped. Thus, we started brainstorming on what the Kannada translation for buttermilk could be.

A few minutes later, my mother hit the jackpot.

She told the waiter – "*Naalu majjige!*" She smiled in triumph.

The waiter nonchalantly went into the kitchen and shouted – "Four buttermilk!"

Language truly crosses boundaries, be it a country or the humble *Benne dosa*.

Chapter 2

CALL OF THE CHOLAS – THE TANJAVUR DIARIES

"Shiva! Get up! What are you doing???? We have a train to catch in 1 hour!"

Fantastic. I had almost made Obama run out.

I got up, groggily, shapes of various objects shifting in and out of focus. My mother was waving a cup of tea in front of my face in desperation. I had been sleeping with my mouth open for the past 4 hours after a very long cricket match...........where I was the scorekeeper.

"Everyone ready?" My father's voice boomed across the hall. My brother was coolly reading the newspaper, already packed and geared up for the trip. Before my father came into my room to check my status quo, I gulped down the tea and rushed into the bathroom. A few minutes later, I was out and raring to go.

For now.

We had ordered our taxi guy to arrive exactly two hours before the arrival of the train. He entered with only one hour to go. My brother and I were about to lift the suitcases to the car when:

"Wait. Did you switch off the geyser?" my brother shouted.

"How should I know? Ask the geyser," I replied coolly.

Apparently this was not the best time to showcase my sense of humour, as my brother rushed upstairs to "contain" the situation. He returned a minute later, his face red, which then turned to a shade of orange. I wondered if green was possible.

"You hadn't switched off the T.V, computer, fan, iron box AND the geyser," he fumed.

"Ah yes. That happened."

Before I could get pounded to pulp, my parents arrived downstairs, with the taxi waiting outside the building. The driver had an expression which was set in stone. He took our luggage without any expression or any explanation as to why he was late. Our luggage was dumped in the backseat as we squeezed ourselves into the tiny car, trying to occupy every inch of it. We had ordered for an SUV but got an excuse for a car. So next time you want a SUV, order a Ferrari.

The traffic was terrible. We had exactly 40 minutes until our train arrived and the driver was showing no signs of hurry. My father was getting impatient by the second.

"Sir, please go a bit fast, we have a train to catch."

"Hm."

He answers only in syllables, it seems.

We were going at an extremely slow pace. Even if a tortoise had a race against us, it would beat us, have lunch, and beat us again. The tortoise analogy was the final straw. I had to take matters into my own hands.

I kept my phone next to my ear and shouted – "What?!!? Rajnikant's at the railway station???"

I don't know why- it just occurred to me to say that. Well, about time. The driver suddenly jerked into action as he slammed the accelerator with full force as we were all thrown backwards. My brother, who was sitting in the front seat, clung on to dear life. My mother screamed and my father couldn't believe was what was going on. He drove with such speed and skill that even John Abraham on his Dhoom bike would be jealous.

We reached the railway station in record time, just enough time for us to walk to the train comfortably. My father was bewildered at the way we had arrived at the station but was extremely amused with my antics. He tipped the driver generously. But the driver was in no mood to even accept money. He kept shouting at the top of his voice:

"Rajni Sir! Where are you?!"

We picked up our bags and started to walk towards our platform. It was a long way to the other side – We had to climb a bridge, shove past a thousand people, accept whatever they had to say about IT people rushing about, and then finally reach our destination.

All this had to be done in less than 2 minutes.

We reached our platform, completely out of breath. I had volunteered to take the heaviest luggage and regretted it immediately. I needed Chota Bheem's laddoo more than ever.

My father asked a bystander – "Has Tanjavur Express arrived?"

The man looked at my father up and down and finally said: "No sir, train is 20 minutes late. Enjoy."

What enjoy? The dog peeing on the track looked more bored than I was.

Anyway, I had no choice. I sat on one of the bags and started to observe my surroundings. As I sat down, something inside the bag poked me. Startled, I got up and saw what it was. It was my brother's new smartphone.

I sat on it anyway.

A man was walking from the opposite side, holding a tea cannister and plastic cups, bellowing the words "Chaiya, Chai" in a singsong tone. Families were gossiping loudly, oblivious of the people around them. Overnight travellers sleeping on the floor snored loudly, awaking a baby who had just fallen asleep. The station master was wandering up and down the platform, holding the red and green flags under his arm, probably thinking whether as to have his wife's home cooked dinner or sample the delicious steaming samosas on sale.

Tough choice.

The next 20 minutes passed on quite uneventfully. The train arrived 30 minutes late, unlike what our honourable bystander told us. We checked our names on the list stuck on the train's side, and reached our compartment. We were just about to keep our bags down when two cockroaches flashed a "WELCOME" board to us. Lovely.

Ignoring them, we kept the bags on our seats and stretched. The cool breeze brushed past our faces as the train started to move. I looked out of the window and noticed numerous vehicles thronging the streets and the countless streetlights blazing through the night. I became restless after a while and so fought with my brother while my parents started gossiping about relatives.

After an hour or so, everyone was silent. Two magical words broke the silence.

"Let's eat, "said my mother.

"Ooh yes!!!" we all said in unison.

My mother carefully opened the packed dinner which she had brought from home. Rice mixed with thick, creamy curd and a dash of breathtaking spicy lemon pickle with some potato chips lay in front of us. We attacked the menu without any further delay.

Over the meal, we talked about a lot of things like school (Luckily, "what are your marks, you are lazy, you get up late" conversations never came up), relative gossip and whether the chicken or the egg came first. This is one incident which will remain with me for the rest of my life: FOOD BRINGS PEOPLE TOGETHER. This goes for anyone, anywhere in the world.

If you want to start an important meeting, always do it over food. Breaking the ice is much, much easier when everyone's tummy is happy and contented. Commenting about the weather is pointless. We aren't British.

After the meal, we all became dormant. My father started reading the paper, my mother took up a novel, and my brother started studying the route map. I did bring a classic, about which I had to write a book review of a minimum of 700 words. 700 words were out of the question. I dozed off even before I read the title.

I was in a deep sleep when I felt someone tap me on the side.

"Ticket".

"Qfnvkklhnrtvm"

"Tickketttt....."

"Wgffegehfgbre".

"Oi! SHOW ME YOUR TICKET!"

He screamed and hit me so hard on my back that I suddenly sat up in shock and hit my head on the ceiling (I was in the top berth) of the train. My eyes focused on the light and then on the ticket collector. He was a short, stout man with a grouchy face. His tummy was the size of his temper. He repeated:

"Ticket."

"I don't have it! It's with my father!" I mumbled in a sleepy tone.

"Am I supposed to know who the father and who the son is?" the ticket collector asked rhetorically.

I whimpered out a reply. "He's over there."

My father fished out our ticket. The collector looked at it and within half a second ticked our names in his register. My God, what a hit.

I had trouble sleeping, with my back still smarting. But in a few minutes, I was snoring again.

Eventually, after a few hours, my parents woke me up. I got down from my bed slowly, but steadily, and made my way towards the washrooms. It was still very dark outside and the train light was quite dim. I almost tripped over a man's leg sticking out in the path way. I brushed my teeth and freshened myself. The cold breeze hit my face like someone had just thrown ice cold water over me. The railway door was open, so I could actually enjoy the scenery and the morning weather.

Tanjavur Express finally reached its destination at 5:30 am. We got down with all our luggage and belongings and started walking towards the taxi stand. On the way:

"Who wants masala tea?" my father asked.

"I drink only green tea with digestive biscuits", I said pompously.

"Ok, no tea then. Lakshmi, Hari, how about you?"

"Yes please, definitely," they chorused.

I gave up. I said: "Uncle, four *chai*", to the local tea guy.

We sipped our tea near the platform. As we did so, warmth slowly entered our bodies. There's really something about having a hot drink on a cold, chilly morning that makes you feel better instantly.

We reached the taxi stand. After some bargaining, we told the driver to take us to our hotel, but before that we asked him to show us some places where we could get a good vegetarian breakfast. We earmarked a few places and made our way to the hotel to get ready for the day.

In Tanjavur, I have to say that breakfast was an extremely gratifying experience. We reached a hotel named – "Tanjavur Tiffanies." We were one of the early birds as my father couldn't resist the pangs of hunger, so NOBODY SHOULD resist the pangs of hunger. So, we reached the restaurant pretty early. My mother needed a recommendation to this place, so she asked a lady nearby:

"*Amma, chaappadu nanna irrukuma?*"She asked in Tamil. (Is the food here good?)

The lady replied enthusiastically. "Oh yes! Best food in Tanjavur! I've been coming here for the past 10 years!"

My mother was convinced. "Hari, Shiva – get a seat for 4", she said.

We took our places. As soon as we took our seat, the waiter started:

"Idly, Vada, Upma, Pongal, Plain Dosa, Masala Dosa, Butter Dosa, poori, coffee, tea, Bournvita, Horlicks, Complan…."

I don't know why, but my brother always has a fascination for something that is not on the menu. He told the waiter - "I want tomato dosa."

The waiter looked at him up and down and said: "Sir, no tomato dosa. Only idly, vada, pongal……….he started off again.

"Ok, ok, enough. Hari, take something which is available now. I'll have a poori. Lakshmi?"

"Idly and Upma."

"Shiva?"

"Poori."

"Hari?"

"Let me think…………………I'll tell you."

From experience, my mother and I could make out when my father's face showed that he was extremely hungry. Now, he was at the breaking point, and my brother was fanning the flames.

Our order came very quickly, and we all had our breakfast with relish.

Which is when my brother decided to order.

"I want a masala dosa."

My father exclaimed - "Now?! The driver will come anytime! Anyway, while we're waiting, I'll order coffee. Waiter! Two coffees, by 2."

Did I mention Tanjavur is famous for its degree coffee?

As I was sipping my coffee, I noticed something strange."Hey, isn't that the lady you had talked to outside?" I asked my mother.

My mother screened the kitchen and was equally shocked. That lady was in the kitchen pouring out the batter for the idlys into the mould.

She was a cook in the kitchen, who had been working at this restaurant for the past 10 years, and was recommending her own food to us.

I really was short of words this time.

Later on, we made a small visit to a famous temple in Tanjavur. While we were exploring the temple premises where there were a few stalls set up, my father became interested in one particular stall, where he wanted to purchase a book on religious practices. As he was about to pay the person, he noticed another book lying on top.

"Which language is this?" he asked, picking up the book.

"I don't know Sir."

"What?! You're selling these books without even knowing which language they've been written in? How are you able to sell your books?"

The stall guy was aghast.

"But the people buying the book will know which language it is written in, no?"

After the temple visit, everyone was in agreement that we needed to unwind. We roamed around our hotel a bit, ate *pakodas* and *vadas* at the local tea store and even went for a movie.

So, our trip to Tanjavur was finally over. No, we never did get time to enjoy a musical concert, for which the place is famous for, but I had my brother at home practicing his Carnatic music. That will suffice.

For Now ☺

~~~ ~~~ ~~~

Chapter 3

CALL OF THE HALWA – THE TIRUNELVELI DIARIES PART 1

The southern district of Tirunelveli in Tamil Nadu is known for its cultural activities. My father and I were taking a trip to our ancestral village about 20 km from Tirunelveli to attend a festival honouring our family god.

I protested at first.

"Who is going to take forward the family traditions? You should come and meet your relatives!" my father thundered.

My brother was preparing for a professional exam, so he escaped with the excuse that he had to study. I, on the other hand, was extremely busy – doing nothing.

"I want to stay at home and watch FRIENDS," I remarked, referring to the famous American sit-com.

"Make new FRIENDS over there. We're going, it's decided."

"No chance. I'm not moving............"

"We can have hot halwa over there."

I stopped talking midway when I heard the word 'halwa'. My mouth started to water.

Tirunelveli Halwa is a sweet delicacy available in............well, Tirunelveli. It is an eclectic mix of many calorie packed ingredients, wheat and ghee being the main culprits. If eating halwa was a sin, I would be a serial offender of the law. I could imagine the halwa being served in the banana leaf, that sinful ball of cashew, cardamom and ghee, right in the centre of my palm. It wobbled in my hand like a bubble, its copper colour shining in the sunlight.

I couldn't wait.

"I'm in. Let's go." I told my father.

A week later, we made our way to the railway station. Unfortunately, my father had caught a cold the day before our journey.

But he was determined to make it to his ancestral village. He used to go there as a little boy to meet his grandfather, and he wasn't in a mood to give this opportunity a miss.

The funniest thing happened. Whenever my dad travels with me, with or without a cold, he always indulges in fried snacks in excess. He just cannot resist them.

"Boss, 2 samosas," he told the vendor.

"Dad, Mom will get to know. She doesn't like you having fried items. It's not good for your health."

"She will get to know.......only if you tell her," Dad gave me a meaningful look.

"Good point." I wolfed down my samosa.

The overnight train journey went without any excitement or furore, except the one time the ticket collector decided to discharge his duties at 12 pm in the middle of the night.

Because everyone would be awake then. Who sleeps at 12 pm?

"Shiva! Get up!"

"Dad.....one more pizza to finish....." I mumbled.

"Tch, tch – brush your teeth, fast. We're reaching in ten minutes."

We reached Tirunelveli at 6 am in the morning. I could have finished my pizza by then.

Which is when my father went berserk.

"Ah! The beautiful morning air! Nothing like home! Wah! *Hindustan ki khushboo!*" (The Fragrance of India)

"Dad, we live in India."

"Shush.....you hungry?"

I stared at him for a full 5 seconds. Neither of us uttered a word.

My father genuinely looked confused at my expression.

"Dad, its 6 am in the morning. Even the rooster near our house would still be sleeping."

"You're not? You should have told me this before hand! I'm FAMISHED."

I made a mental note that his cold had disappeared.

He took me to a roadside restaurant. The proprietor placed two identical plates in front of us. It had 3 pooris (Indian fried bread), a vada (savoury fried snack), chutney and a lump of potato masala serving as the side-kick to the poori.

Note: The added explanations in brackets are for our foreign friends who may not know much about Indian cuisine. Also included in the above category are ABCD(American Born Confused Desi's). The rest of you can continue reading.

"Poori? Vada? Fried items at 6 am in the morning? What will Mom say?" I exclaimed loudly.

"I can have your share, if you like," my father offered.

10 MINUTES LATER

"The poori was delicious, but the vada could have been a bit more crispier," I thought.

We packed six onion vadas to eat on the way, just in case we got hungry again. In our household, food takes priority over everything else.

After a beautiful thirty minute bus ride on the highway, we reached our destination.

My father's relative came to receive us.

"Shankaraaaa! How are you? Such a long time it's been!"

My father grinned in response.

"So, this is Shiva! Good, good – you brought your son along too!"

"He wanted to learn about our family traditions, rituals and culture. I told him it would be boring, only gossip and hot afternoons – but he was determined to come." My father said with a straight face.

If it wasn't for the halwa....

The relative looked at me in admiration.

"Did you have breakfast? It's already 8 in the morning!"

"No, we haven't eaten anything since yesterday night. Right, Shiva?"

"Liar, liar – pants on fire," said the poori in my stomach.

My father was fighting hard to suppress his smile.

"Yes, of course. Dinner was our last meal since we arrived." I kept up our stance.

I hid the empty vada packet behind my back.

Chapter 4

THE HUNGER GAMES – THE TIRUNELVELI DIARIES PART 2

It was 6 am in the morning, and I had already had a bath.

Imagine you're in a deep slumber, in a magical place, drifting into nothingness – when suddenly someone dumps a bucket of ice-cold water on you.

I come from a Tamil-Brahmin family (Tam-Brahm), so festivals and functions always start at the break of dawn. When I was forced to wake up from my deep sleep, I brushed my teeth and immediately gulped down a glass of piping hot filter coffee.

Filter coffee is to Tam-Brahms what water is to plants. It can be, and will be consumed at any time of the day, irrespective of the amount consumed.

Tam-Brahm's have filter coffee before breakfast, during breakfast, after breakfast, before lunch, after lunch, and in the evening with some savouries and snacks. The coffee market has been booming since the start of time, and the credit should go solely to us.

I was in a village environment, so I used to spend my time chasing roosters and goats, because exercise is important. The village dogs chased me, because they had no other work to do.

My dad and I were ready by 6:30 am, and so were the others. It was the day of the festival, the day our family deity would be honoured.

There is a recurring problem which has been haunting my family for many years now. I call it – The Hunger Games. A conspicuous term, no doubt. I believe that Hunger plays a cat and mouse game with the human stomach, leading or rather coercing the said human to take action with immediate effect.

In simple terms – irrespective of the time of the day, be it 4 am in the morning or 12 pm in the night, we would feel the pangs of hunger haunting us. My father and I have caught the mentioned disease several times but yet continue to ignore its symptoms.

The disease reared its ugly head again today morning.

"Shiva, let's have some vada."
"Dad, breakfast is at 9 am."
"I can't wait for that long."
"Neither can I. Let's go."

We started to walk towards the vada shop, about a kilometre away, when we heard a voice in the distance.

"Shankar! Where are you going?"

A group of elders had stopped us on the way. They were seated on the front porch of an ancestral house. One sipped his filter coffee, smacking his lips, while the two others looked at us suspiciously.

Filter Coffee's eyes narrowed down on us.

"Oh! Nowhere really......I thought I'd take my son for a walk to the family temple."

I suppressed my laughter.

"The Puja does not start until 10 am. What are you going to do over there?" Filter Coffee asked.

"Prayers should be done early in the morning, right? I wanted my son to learn some good habits while he is here."

I was busy counting the number of vadas I could eat at one go in my head. I estimated 10, at the most.

"But the temple is 3 km away. Why do you want to walk that distance?"

"Why not? I needed the exercise anyway," my father laughed nervously.

"Let us be, we want to gobble up some vadas," I pleaded mentally to Filter Coffee.

"Hmmmm.....ok. On your way then." Filter Coffee released us.

My father and I merrily walked down the path towards the vada shop. Everyone was hungry early in the morning, but no one would admit it for fear of being admonished by their fellow community members. My father and I hardly cared.

We were halfway into our journey when:

"*Arre* Shankar! There you are! Come, we are also going to the temple! We'll drop you and your son over there!" Filter Coffee said, and grinned.

Filter Coffee and his two henchmen had arrived in an autorickshaw. We had no choice, but to comply. Our plan had been foiled.

Bye, Bye vada.

But the joke was on us. We reached the temple premises, prayed to the family deity for a few minutes, and immediately, out of the blue, we heard a voice:

"Breakfast is ready!"

It goes without saying, my father and I had the time of our lives wolfing down steaming hot *Upma* (a thick porridge from dry roasted semolina or coarse rice flour) and sambar.

Was it in our fate to see the deity and then have our breakfast? What if we had managed to avoid the autorickshaw?

Do we really have control over our lives? Or is everything decided before hand?

PROVIDENCE.........or COINCIDENCE?

www.ingramcontent.com/pod-product-compliance
Lightning Source LLC
Chambersburg PA
CBHW022117040426
42450CB00006B/735